A Welsh Odyssey

A Welsh Odyssey

CHILDHOOD, EXILE AND THE SEARCH FOR THE HIRAETH INSIDE

JOS SIMON

y Lolfa

First impression: 2025

© Copyright Jos Simon and Y Lolfa Cyf., 2025

The contents of this book are subject to copyright, and may
not be reproduced by any means, mechanical or electronic,
without the prior, written consent of the publishers.

Cover design: Y Lolfa
Cover image: Simon van de Put

ISBN: 978 1 80099 641 0

Published and printed in Wales
on paper from well-maintained forests by
Y Lolfa Cyf., Talybont, Ceredigion SY24 5HE
website www.ylolfa.com
e-mail ylolfa@ylolfa.com
tel 01970 832 304

Contents

Introduction

TO BEGIN AT the beginning…

In 2013 a Facebook group called *Ysgolion Pwllheli and District Schools* was launched. Membership, as its name suggests, was limited to people who had at some point in the past attended either of Pwllheli's two secondary schools or the primary schools that fed them. I joined the group soon after it was established.

YPDS became an online meeting place where we could swap anecdotes, share photographs, mull over stories of the past, indulge in a bit of banter, or remind ourselves of people who'd left – either Pwllheli, or Llŷn, or indeed this mortal coil. Posts, and the responses to them, were wide-ranging and sometimes very funny. 'Why not assemble them into a book?' someone eventually suggested.

Why not indeed? So that's what we did.

The book was published in 2022 as *On Bonfires, Butlins and Being Welsh: Growing Up in Pwllheli in the '50s and '60s*.

That's that, I thought.

But to my surprise, the memories, my own and those of other members of the group, didn't stop. They kept coming. As they did so, I spent many hours at my keyboard, once again reliving my childhood, dashing the odd sentimental tear from my eye or, more often, chuckling and guffawing over the stories of what we did, where, and with whom. And these further stories led to thoughts of how being Welsh affected us for the rest of our lives. The stories begged to be included in a sequel. *A Welsh Odyssey* is that sequel.

At the heart of both books are these stories. For the ones in *On Bonfires, Butlins and Being Welsh* (the curse of the severed hand, for example, or my brother falling off Pwllheli's gasometer) you'll need to read the book (still in print and available from the publisher and from all good bookshops!).

But there are loads of new stories in this sequel – stories about young model-makers high on glue, about a Trefor garden-shed poison-making factory, about the deserved hangover torments of local university students, about the battle between a group of small boys and the moon. And many more.

When I grew up I left Pwllheli for a life and career outside Wales. As did lots of members of our Facebook group. In my case, I didn't move far – never more than a few hundred miles away in England. Others fetched up much further afield – in Ireland, Denmark, Germany, Canada, Australia, the USA, China and elsewhere. But like them I suspect, my links with my homeland continued, sometimes fading, sometimes flourishing. An account of the ebb and flow of these links, and the *hiraeth* that drove them, completes this second book.

My first book went down well, but if there was a practical criticism from my friends it was that it took an awfully long time to get going.

Fair enough. This time I'll just shut up and crack on.

Part One

More Tales From Pwllheli And Llŷn

Memoirist Blake Morrison has observed that, when you revisit the past, you find new things each time you go there – things you missed or didn't understand or failed to see the significance of, which as you get older you begin to grasp.

Spot on. This is exactly what happened to us members of the *Ysgolion Pwllheli and District Schools* Facebook group. So the stories continued to flood in.

But they're not just stories. Taken as a whole, for me at least, they formed a mental comfort blanket, something that consoled me when I was crippled by home-sickness and, even when I thought I'd forgotten all about my Welsh upbringing, was still there in the background for the rest of my life.

So here's that comfort blanket – a patchwork quilt of the things we did, the places we did them in, and the people we did them with.

CHAPTER 1

Things we did

Model-making

I recently realised that, threaded unnoticed through the crests and troughs of childhood and adolescence, was a protected oasis of calm, a safe place to which I could withdraw and recharge my batteries.

Making models.

Why do boys (and it usually *is* boys) like making models? I Googled the question, but the responses – largely from across the Atlantic – were less than helpful. Along the lines of 'Why guys really want to "make" models'. And I'm cleaning up the language here. I'd forgotten that 'make', and indeed 'models', can mean different things in Britain and the United States.

My initiation into model-making came when I was at primary school. I was ill, and Dad bought me an Airfix model of the *Cutty Sark*. To give me something to do. I was immediately hooked. I soon moved on to my loves – aircraft. The Sopwith Camel, the Gloucester Gladiator, the Westlands Lysander, the Mosquito, the Spitfire, and – my favourite (and biggest) model – the Lancaster Bomber.

A box, a plastic spine with parts attached, a tube of glue and an instruction sheet. Bliss. To start with I'd go at it like a bull at a gate, and end up with glue all over my fingers, moving parts that wouldn't move, and bits left over at the end. When I was

11

older, I'd be more careful. Take the Lancaster. The propellors would spin, the guns move, the turrets rotate and the wheels revolve. I even painted the plane and attached the red, white and blue RAF 'roundels'. My only sorrow was that, for all that I hung it from the ceiling of my bedroom on a fishing line, it couldn't actually fly.

So I embarked on Phase two – balsa-wood light aircraft with rubber-band-driven propellors. Again, parts attached to a spine, but this time balsa-wood rather than plastic. I'd study the plans, lay out the parts, build and glue. Then, when it was all finished, I'd stretch the elastic band from the wire hook behind the engine-block-mounted propellor to the end of the fuselage near the tail, wind the prop round and round, and launch my creation into the sky. On a wing and a prayer. And it flew! I was proud of those planes.

Phase three beckoned – a glider with a four-foot wingspan. I built the balsa-wood framework on the big table next to the back window of my bedroom. In sections, held down with pins. Then I glued the whole shebang together and covered it in tissue paper. Finally, I coated this increasingly impressive structure in yellow dope. When dried, my plane looked – amazing!

I carried it up onto the Garn, the hill above Pwllheli, for its maiden flight. Coddling it, I climbed to the summit. There was a stiff breeze in off Cardigan Bay – just right to ensure the necessary lift. The town and the harbour lay below, the sea sparkling in the distance, the mountains beyond. I held my beautiful plane high up above my head, facing into the wind. I felt exultant.

With a crack, both wings broke off. Snapped backwards and slapped against the fuselage, held only by the flimsy doped tissue paper.

Fighting tears, I stamped back down off the Garn, down into town, back to the house. Months of work down the drain. Our dustbin stood outside the house waiting to be emptied. I lifted the lid and crunched the broken glider viciously down in among the rubbish where it belonged. I stormed into the house. My mother called out to me, but I ignored her, and sprinted up both flights of stairs to my attic bedroom. I swept all the construction detritus – the bits of balsa-wood, the pins, the strips of tissue paper, the empty dope bottles and glue tubes, the paper blueprints – onto the floor. Then I threw myself onto my bed and cried. And cried.

So perhaps model-making wasn't quite the oasis I remember. But still, I'm sure that, for child model-makers like myself, and for all other enthusiasts – train-spotters, bird-watchers, surfers, petrol-heads, football-supporters, philatelists – our hobbies give us a respite from the knotty confusion and difficult relationships of the real world.

What's not to like?

Model-making – postscript

Inevitably, most of the comments came from boys (by now, of course, old men):

- The impatience of one led to the use of inappropriate glue in a model plane supplied free in *The Eagle* comic. The resulting maiden flight, attended by family and friends, ended in disaster – a spectacular crash. The builder's despair was further deepened when he overheard his mother saying to the rest of the onlookers, 'So Garry won't be joining the RAF then!'

- The only female contributor, living vicariously through four male cousins, was able to describe in detail their model-making mania. Their interests ranged widely, from plasticine to Meccano to balsa-wood to Airfix. Their bedrooms were obstacle-courses of completed aircraft, hanging from the ceiling, and construction took up all the living room easy chairs (with their materials spread out on planks spanning the chair-arms), so that parents and visitors were forced to perch at the dining table. The appeal for the boys, she noted, was clearly in process rather than product – when the models were finished they lost interest.

- Finally, in different contributions, the reasons for the popularity of model-making were intriguingly hinted at. Parents encouraged it because it kept normally boisterous boys quiet for hours, while boys enjoyed it not only for the pride in the finished model, but also because of the pleasant psychedelic effects of the glue fumes.

School projects

From the amateur efforts of child hobbyists, earnestly applying themselves in bedrooms or dining rooms or living rooms, to the far more serious output of carefully crafted artefacts, created in classrooms, guided by teachers.

Yes, the stuff we made in school.

Any parent or grandparent will tell you, I'm sure, that the steady stream of things that the kids have made in school – paintings, pots, projects, models, stories, calendars – are, how can I put this – a mixed blessing. You love to get them, to see the shy pride with which they're offered. You display them, attach them to the fridge, hang them on the wall. But then what?

You do your best. If space allows, you might add them to a memory box in the loft. But sometimes they do 'get lost'. And when they do, you wouldn't be human if you didn't heave a small, secret, sigh of relief.

None of the stuff I made at school has survived. I'm not complaining. My parents' generation, I suspect, was a lot less sentimental than ours. When they were growing up they had other things to worry about, like the lack of an NHS, the absence of free education, mass unemployment, the Great Depression and two world wars.

So my memories are stored not in the loft but in my head.

From primary school I remember taking home:

- A calendar I made one Christmas in Miss Jones's class. This is my most vivid memory – a rectangle of card with a picture of a cat sitting on a wall among rooftops and chimney-stacks, silhouetted against a huge moon (all made from shapes cut out of different coloured squares of sticky paper), with the tiny shop-bought calendar dangling underneath. I was hugely proud of it, and it hung on a nail next to the kitchen range in our house for the whole of the following year.

- A small clay model of an Airedale terrier. Not fired – this was long before Dad installed a kiln at school. It lived on a windowsill, also in the kitchen.

- A puppet with a papier-mâché head and a 'glove' made of fabric offcuts. It was joined, at home, by several more puppets, together with a home-made cardboard theatre. Neither puppets nor theatre survived for long, and no plays were ever written or performed. Shakespeare's ghost can rest easy.

Because of specialist teaching and well-equipped craft rooms, the production values of my secondary school output skyrocketed:

- A wooden clothes hook (which ended up holding my dressing gown on the back of my bedroom door).

- A teapot stand (which for a while graced the kitchen table, until it didn't).

- A rack of chunky coasters (similar fate to the teapot stand).

- A garden fork (small, for use in pots or window boxes). We had neither pots nor window boxes, so it died not only in obscurity, but a virgin.

- A toolmaker's clamp (the most professional-looking of the things I made, but the least useful. I had no idea what it was for, and, let's face it, I was never likely to be making any tools).

15

The first three were made in woodwork, the last two in metalwork. Though, the fork *handle* (no *Two Ronnies* jokes please) was made of wood, turned by me on a lathe.

I now understand, from the lofty heights of old age, that all those early lessons were designed to develop specific skills:

- In woodwork, the making of joints – cross-halving (the teapot stand), dovetail (the toast-rack) and mortise and tenon (the clothes hook) – together with the more general skills of measuring, marking-out, sawing, planing, sanding, hammering.

- In metalwork the endless cutting and filing of mild steel sheets (the garden fork) and metal lathe-turning (the clamp). Some of this required the use of a bastard file – I remember Jack Wood announcing its name with a challenging glint in his eye and a belligerent jut to his jaw, daring anybody to laugh.

To turn to the experience of my older brother Jeff. He spent a year in Form Six before going off to college, and was given a lot of workshop time with Jack – to fill up his timetable, I suspect. That's Jeff's timetable, not Jack's. I suspect, too, that he was told to design and build anything he thought might be useful at home, just to keep him out of mischief. They could do that sort of thing in those days.

I can remember with absolute clarity the two rather impressive results:

- A picnic table for Mum. It was made of a red wood (Mahogany? An expensive hardwood? Surely not!), with a yellow formica top, beading to stop the dishes sliding off and two H-shaped legs which folded away underneath. It was heavy (so perhaps it *was* mahogany), and was really well-designed and well-made.

- A golf trolley for Dad. Impressively big, it could be collapsed into the boot of the car with his clubs. It was black, very functional, and made of mild steel, or perhaps wrought iron.

But I also think that my brother's experience points to a more important truth. It wasn't just about skills, it was about pride, it was about heart:

- The picnic table was a hit – no question. We used it for years until it disappeared.
- The golf trolley, I'm not so sure. Dad certainly used it. But mature reflection leads me to two conclusions:
  - o Jeff, amidst fraught relations with our father over school work (or lack of it), coming home late at night, and general adolescent bloody-mindedness, spent weeks designing and making him a golf trolley. Surely this speaks volumes about his underlying if reluctant love for his dad. Deeds, not words.
  - o Dad continued to use the trolley – one that looked like a First World War howitzer and weighed almost as much – for years, despite the fact that I bet other sleek-trollied club-members mercilessly took the mickey. Surely this speaks volumes about his exasperated love for his eldest son. Again, deeds, not words.

That's the great pleasure of writing posts for Facebook. You start by describing a calendar that you made when you were seven, and end up analysing the generation gap as illustrated by the relationship between your adolescent elder brother and his (your) dad!

As the Americans say, 'Go figure!'

School projects – postscript

This post generated several heartfelt responses:

1. The most surprising for me was a group member who said that he and his sister had for many years (between the ages of one and eight) eaten at my brother's picnic table, and said that it was a lovely thing, ideal for two small children to sit at, together, on the floor. When I queried how this had come about, he had no idea. Perhaps, we thought, it had been given to his parents by my parents,

or that my parents had donated it to a jumble sale and his parents had bought it. I hope the former rather than the latter. But at least I now know where it went.

2. My friend Tony Pierce remembers *his* coat hook as being vastly superior to mine, but when he showed it proudly to his mother was deflated by her verdict – 'It's not very good, is it?' Clearly a lady of refined taste, if a little flinty of heart.

3. One particular comment was amusing and touching on several levels. A standard lamp made in school failed to stand up properly, mainly because its base consisted of an old office chair with a buttock-shaped indentation. When, frustrated by the lamp's refusal to stop wobbling, he suggested to his mother that it be sent to auction, she wouldn't hear of it. 'If we did that, what would I have to remember my first-born's work,' she said. Looking back, he felt that he'd been gullible to believe her. Not gullible but innocent. And what a tribute to his mother's love and sensitivity. And sense of humour!

4. My younger brother's contribution to this postscript didn't, I'm afraid, reflect well on me. He claimed that I had form as a 'puppet murderer'. I'd stepped, apparently, on the ceramic head of a (bought) puppet that he was very proud of, smashing it to bits. He howled. I promised to make a new head for it, 'good as new'. The replacement I made consisted of the blue tube from the centre of a ball of string with a face biro'd onto it. Again he howled, even louder. Needless to say, I have no memory of this dark episode.

5. Finally, a member of the group said that nothing ('zilch') that she'd made at Trefor Primary School had survived. However, a member of staff ('an early-years hoarder') had preserved her diary ('*dyddlyfr*') presumably filled-in at school. Two entries for 1966 she felt were particularly

noteworthy. The first recorded the death of her much-loved grandfather ('*taid* New Street'), the second the horrors of the Aberfan disaster. In each case what was remarkable was the clear-eyed, unemotional deadpan delivery: '*Mae Taid Brenda wedi marw*' ('Brenda's grandfather has died'). Followed by a factual report of the Aberfan disaster – number of deaths, day-by-day news, the funerals and the class collection made for the victims. Not a mention of her reaction to the horror. I really don't know what to make of this. Are kids unemotional 'midwich cuckoos'? Or do they simply report trauma, then suffer the effects of it for the rest of their lives? The latter, surely.

From disappointment to despair

I've posted a few times about the disappointments and frustrations of my childhood – of that first flight of a glider I'd built being aborted (I never forgave God for that – see above). Of a gust of wind destroying an altar that at six years old I'd built in the garden (God's fault again – see below). Of not getting (at ages eleven to sixteen) the watch, or bike, or guitar, that I really really wanted (in each case, Dad's fault – see further below). In all of these setbacks I vividly remember how upset I'd been.

But when, in my late teens, I was working on Dick Parry's speedboats, I heard a story that was hard to beat for – disappointment's not a strong enough word. Despair? I heard about it second or third hand and I may have got the details wrong, but it has haunted me ever since.

The story concerned a large and hansome cabin cruiser that was being launched from a slipway at Baines boatyard in Pwllheli. It had been built by a businessman from somewhere near Manchester, and was his pride and joy. It had taken him over two years of planning, of buying materials, of learning new skills and of hard daily graft, to build it in a barn which he'd rented for the purpose. It was luxuriously appointed, was equipped with powerful engines, and had every navigation aid known to man. It was his dream to leave the cares of everyday life behind and sail the world's oceans. It was a noble ambition which any of us, even non-nauticals like myself, could only admire.

Finally, when the last bit of kit had been installed, the last lick of varnish applied and all the documentation completed, it was transported to Pwllheli, to be launched and taken through its paces out on Cardigan Bay.

As the cradle bearing its precious cargo inched down the slipway, there was a loud crack. The keel of the boat had snapped.

In the weeks and months that followed, every effort was made to repair the boat. This was partly successful. But it was never going to be the ocean-going thoroughbred that it's owner and builder had dreamed of. It was confined to plodding along inshore waters and inland waterways.

The spectrum of disappointments/frustrations/devastations we all suffer in life range from the relatively trivial to the horribly serious, from being pipped for a parking space to seeing your team just miss promotion to getting a terminal diagnosis.

But there was something about this story that has stayed with me for over half a century. I can't imagine what the builder of that boat felt when the keel snapped and the bow and stern sagged.

God, they say, looks at our plans and laughs. He must be a sadist.

I'm pretty sure this is a true story, though I may have embelished it or invented some of the details.

From disappointment to despair – postscript

My memory of the outlines of the story was confirmed by several members of the group. And the two main comments were among the most uplifting that I've had the pleasure to receive or write about:

- One was a story of comeuppance, of karma. It was the tale of a fishing boat bought, after its owner had died, from the distraught widow by an unscrupulous buyer for a pittance. When the deal had been closed and the money had changed hands, the boat was cradled out of the water. 'The keel sickeningly cracked and the whole hull sagged.' The death of a boat is not usually a cause for celebration, but in this case you'd find it hard not to cheer!

- Even more inspirational was a comment from the son of the 1960s owner of Baines boatyard, who said that the builder of the 'brokeback' cabin cruiser that I'd written about turned up at the yard years later with another cabin-cruiser, again one that he'd built himself. This one remained unscathed and was launched without incident. It's name? The *Second Chance*! From disappointment, through despair, to triumph!

Indomitable or what?

Teen-communications

By and large, my parents approved of Arthur Mee's ten-volume *Children's Encyclopaedia*. They must have done – they bought the whole set for my brother Jeff and me. And we used it a lot, especially when it was raining. But one of the 'Things to make and do' eventually gave them some grief.

The relevant section was about creating a telephone with a length of string and two tin cans. It was simple – you attached a tin can to either end of the string, pulled it tight, and spoke. And it worked! Jeff and I tried it in the garden with longer and longer lengths of string, and it continued to work.

We were ecstatic.

But we wanted to extend it even further. My bedroom was

in the attic of the main terraced house, Jeff's was on the floor below, in the bit that stuck out into the garden. So we tried to create a phone from his bedroom to mine. It didn't work, because the string, after leaving his bedroom window, had to stretch up and over the roof to mine. This change of direction, with the string pulled tight against the slate of the roof-edge, stopped it working.

We were crestfallen.

Uncle Owen, my mother's older brother, to the rescue. Seeing our disappointment, he chipped in with some advice. 'What you need,' he said, 'is some headphones, some wire and a battery.'

At this time – not long after the end of the Second World War – *Exchange and Mart* was flooded with army-surplus equipment. My brother and I immediately pooled our pocket money, dispatched an order for headphones, bought one of those big, blue square batteries and a spool of wire (from Woolworths, I think), and were soon up and running.

The solid Bakelite earcups of the headphones were detachable. With one in my bedroom and the other in Jeff's, and the two joined to each other (and to the battery) via a length of wire across the roof, we conversed. We spoke and listened. Loud and clear!

Next problem? How did we call one another up?

Solution? A piece of string (in fact, the same one we used for our failed tin-can telephone) between our two bedrooms.

The alert? On Jeff's end, an old alarm clock with the cover removed. The string was tied to a bent arm which dropped into a spring-loaded cog-wheel. A yank on the string would lift the arm, allow the cog-wheel to rotate, and the bell to ring. At my end, we didn't have another alarm clock, so my alert was a tin can (yes, again recycled from the TCT) full of marbles. If Jeff tugged the string, the tin would jiggle, rattling the marbles.

It worked. Jeff could call me, I could call him. Often in the middle of the night. We could chat companionably as we smoked out of our respective windows, doing impressions of racing cars, or complaining about our parents.

Then, at two in the morning, the string broke. The tin can crashed to my bedroom floor, and marbles scattered far and wide all over the hard brown lino. Mum and Dad, who slept in the room directly below, burst in looking frightened and half-asleep. They found me in my pyjamas trying to keep my footing while desperately chasing marbles hither and yon.

To be fair, neither Mum nor Dad really gave us any grief. They were quite proud of our enterprise. Or so I like to think.

It's easier nowadays. Kids just use their mobile phones.

Teen-communications – postscript

One member of the group's similar experiment with a tin can telephone system came from a different source – the Ladybird book *Things to make or do*. It worked impressively from the house to a caravan at the end of the garden.

There followed a lamentation that the youth of today is deprived of that drive to dismantle things to see how they work. Everything today seems to be inaccessible. As I discovered when I tried to replace a headlamp bulb on my car – it was a sealed-beam unit.

Hare-brained schemes

I'm sure that the young throughout history have indulged in hare-brained schemes. They're part of early years' education, part of growing up. They're not even restricted to the human young – anybody with a dog or cat or who's seen documentaries about lionesses and their cubs will have seen them in action. And sometimes – think of the fledgling plummeting to earth – they can be fatal.

In comparison, my own hare-brained schemes were pretty tame.

Maps

The old public-school explanation of the difference between geography and history ('Geography is about maps; History is about chaps') is not only sexist, but oversimplified. Yet there's no denying that maps fascinate kids. I can't count the number of times during my childhood that I (and friends) drew maps. Maps of imaginary treasure islands, maps of our rooms, of our houses, of our street, of our town. I can remember drawing maps of Pwllheli, but I never got it quite right. However careful I was, the final streets never quite connected properly. It reminds me, sixty years later, of one of my grandchildren trying to draw a picture, and rejecting each effort with, 'It's too big,' then, 'It's too small,' finally, furiously, 'It's too medium.'

Clubs

Kids create innumerable clubs or societies. It's a way, I suppose, of being exclusive – as long as you belong to the club and it excludes other people, it makes you feel good. It really doesn't matter what the club is for – gardening (see next section), bird watching, doing puppet-shows behind W H Smiths. What is important is that it has a constitution, rules, membership cards, and possibly initiation ceremonies. None of the clubs for which I wrote constitutions and rules ever saw the light of day – they were confined to my head. But look around – the driving force (from workingmen's clubs to golf clubs to Whites or the Athenaeum) is there for all to see.

Pethau Plannu

Around the back in the playground outside Miss Jones's classroom in Penlleiniau, next to the end of the school-house, was a discarded toilet bowl, full of soil. I've no idea why it was there – it wasn't connected to anything. I and several friends in Miss Jones's class – we must have been seven or eight years old – decided to make it the basis for a gardening club which we called *Pethau Plannu*. We didn't have gardens of our own, so this would have to do. In lieu. (Oh, please!) We chipped in from our pocket money and bought a packet of seeds from Woolworths – Sweet William. We planted the seeds and waited with bated breath for the inevitable explosion of flowers, as shown on the packet. When they didn't immediately shoot out of the soil, we lost interest and moved on to the next scheme. I don't know if Sweet William ever put in an appearance. When my parents moved into the school-house over twenty years later, there was no sign of the flowers. Or, come to think of it, the toilet bowl.

The altar

As a child, like many of us, I briefly went through a religious phase. It lasted most of an afternoon. I decided to build an altar in the garden at which I could worship the creator.

I found an old fruit crate in the shed, a length of cloth in the middle-room cupboard where Dad hoarded stuff he said he was going to use in school but never did, a small vase on a shelf in the scullery, and some silver paper I'd rescued from empty Churchmans No. 1 cigarette packets in the dustbin. I assembled my finds at the far end of the garden (as far away from the house as I could get: I certainly didn't want big brother Jeff making fun) and built the altar against the wall between our garden and Frondeg School's yard.

I settled the crate into the long grass, draped it with the cloth, set up the vase with water from the scullery and a bunch of wild flowers (there were no others on offer – Dad was no gardener), then made little goblets from the silver paper. I didn't have a cross, but this would have to do. As I settled down with eyes closed, hands together and head bowed in prayer, a gust of wind blew away the silver cups and tipped the vase over.

I was incensed! How could God allow this to happen when I'd gone to all this trouble? I angrily kicked the altar further into the long grass, said uncomplimentary things about the deity, and stomped off to find something more rewarding to do.

The rocket tin

The month after I started secondary school Sputnik was launched into orbit. I became interested in space exploration. Time, I thought, for Wales to enter the space race. I'd found a small flat oblong tin that had contained little black throat sweets called Nigroids. The racist overtones were lost on me.

In my bedroom I punched a row of holes along one of the short sides, soaked a rag in lighter fuel I'd found in Dad's bureau, then tucked it (the rag, not the bureau) into the tin. The plan was to set fire to the cloth and snap shut the lid. This, I imagined, would lead to a jet of flame issuing out of the holes I'd made, driving the improvised rocket (in accordance with Newton's laws of motion) in the opposite direction, out of the window.

Nothing of the sort of course happened. The cloth caught fire, but so did the fuel on my hands. I dropped the tin, still open, onto the bed, and luckily had the presence of mind to smother the flames with the eiderdown.

I assume I must have thought up a convincing explanation for the blackened holes in the bedding and the scorch marks on my hands, but after sixty-five years I honestly can't remember what they were.

To this day my family have no idea how my bravery and quick-thinking saved them from a fiery death.

A meteorological experiment

Having read an article about the weather in Arthur Mee's *Children's Encyclopaedia* – specifically about rainfall – I decided to check his conclusions. This involved collecting rainfall statistics for Llys Pedr in Pwllheli's Llŷn Street. Our house.

I waited until it was raining (no flies on me) and settled myself at my bedroom window – thankfully the one that looked out over the back of the house towards Frondeg School, not the one high above Llŷn Street. The window was a dormer, which opened outwards, and I held the collecting flask (a rose-pink vase made of very thin glass) out into the developing downpour. Of course, it immediately slipped out of my wet hand, plummeted downwards giving off a banshee scream like a bomb falling from a diving Stuka, and detonated in the concrete area between the middle-room, the kitchen and the scullery. An area that, according to my younger brother, my mother later painted white and touchingly christened 'The Patio'.

To my relief, Dad, when we met on the stairs, looked more frightened than angry, and when I explained what I'd been doing, even seemed not only relieved but rather proud of my scientific endeavours. Or (yet again) so I like to think.

Investigative journalism

Into my teens, my friends and I were getting a bit bored hanging out in the loft above Dafydd Bodlew's dad's veterinary practice. True, we had easy chairs, soft drinks (I don't remember any booze), magazines, a wind-up gramophone, and a safe place to smoke. But we needed something more. Had we been in a Hollywood movie, somebody would no doubt have shouted 'Let's put on a show'. But we weren't, and nobody did. However, somebody did suggest that we put together a newspaper. This we *could* do.

It was hand-written and hand-illustrated, with text and pictures glued onto a large sheet of card. Each edition (OK, there was only the one) consisted of jokes and... er... more jokes. Also an ad for W H Smiths (strapline – 'Whatever the weather, Smith's boys deliver') and a weak crossword puzzle.

'We need something more substantial,' Dafydd Bodlew said. He was the editor. His dad *was* our landlord, after all.

We concluded that what was required was some hard-hitting investigative journalism, something that would make the world sit up and take notice. We scratched our heads, and finally came up with a corker.

This was early in December, and the town's Christmas lights had recently appeared above the main streets. 'Have you seen how many bulbs are duds,' somebody said. 'It's a disgrace!' So we divvied up the streets and set off, notebooks and pencils in hand.

Having returned to base and collated the results, we concluded that ten per cent of the bulbs were not lit. It was a scandal – ratepayers were being short-changed. We wrote our exposé, fitted it onto the first edition's front (OK, only) page, fired off stiff letters to the council and the *Caernarfon and Denbigh Herald*, and sat back, waiting for the storm of publicity, the interest from the nationals, the demands for TV interviews.

Neither the council nor the local paper responded. The national and international media remained blithely unconcerned. But we weren't too downhearted. Local coffee-bar Brexo had just been refurbished (with booths and, I think, a new jukebox), and we were keen to see if we approved.

Hare-brained schemes – postscript

I was delighted that I wasn't the only instigator of hare-brained schemes:

- I said at the beginning that mine were pretty tame. And so it transpired. One of the responses – from Maldwyn's daughter (Maldwyn was a senior teacher at YRP) – takes the biscuit for sheer sinister (to use her own word) eccentricity. She created a 'poison-making factory' in the back garden 'cwt bach' of their home in Trefor. This involved dead-heading her father's dahlias, steeping the results in water, waiting until they'd rotted down, then bottling the foul-smelling result. Her father viewed this strange hobby with impressive equanimity. As well he might. Not only did it keep his child (or was it children? She said 'we'. I envisaged a browbeaten younger brother bending to the will of his cackling sibling, an Igor to her Victor Frankenstein) occupied, but it simultaneously reduced the amount of work he had to do in the garden.

- This postscript led to another comment which I found very affecting, from somebody who lived in Trefor at the time. Maldwyn's dahlias, he said, were glorious: *'Dipyn o sioe bob blwyddyn'* ('a bit of show every year').

- Another interesting response included the building of a rabbit hutch from an old piano. 'It didn't work,' the contributor commented sadly. I bet it sounded good, though.

Drinks

Finally, no description of growing up (on Llŷn, certainly, but I would guess anywhere in the world) would be complete without an account of what we drank. I'll divide it into the stuff we drank as little kids, and what we graduated to during adolescence.

Childhood drinks

My brother Chris, a fervent Manchester City fan, treated me a year or two back to an evening match at the Etihad. (For anyone who wishes to pin down the date, it was Yaya Touré's final appearance). On our way from his favourite pub to the tram station, we passed the Vimto memorial, a monument in oak to the famous drink, one of the many things that Manchester is noted for, like the Anti-Corn Law League, the works of Marx and Engels, the Hallè Orchestra and Oasis. This sparked thoughts about other soft drinks from those times. I'll give pride of place to Vimto, then go on to others that I remember:

- Vimto: After the match, thinking it was a hoot, I posted a picture of the Vimto memorial on Facebook, wondering why anybody would erect a statue to a bottle of pop. My Dubai-based son immediately chipped in with something I didn't know – Vimto's very very popular in the Emirates, especially during Ramadan. And all this brought back a further memory – the free booklets of sporting achievements that Vimto used to produce, like thin (and free) versions of the *Guinness Book of Records*, but with no links to the demon alcohol. Furthermore, I was later disappointed to learn from my daughter, that the 'Cheeky Vimto' much favoured by Welsh diva Charlotte Church in fact contains no Vimto – it's a cocktail of port and blue WKD. It owes its name not to its contents but, apparently, to its colour. Who on earth would pollute a fine fortified wine like port with penetrating oil, I asked. She explained that WKD is a type of vodka. The penetrating oil is WD-40. You learn something new every day.

- Lucozade: A straw-coloured liquid contained in a bottle wrapped in straw-coloured cellophane, this was usually to be found on hospital bedside tables, next to bunches of grapes. Although its restorative properties had presumably led to its widespread popularity at a pick-me-up for invalids, I'd have thought there was a danger of confusing it with what often drains out of hospital patients into polythene bags. Perhaps the manufacturers thought so too – they expanded into sports and energy drinks, presumably to get their product associated with health rather than sickness. And they introduced more youthful, more vibrant, less urinary, colours.

- Corona: In my memory, Corona came in a variety of flavours, contained in bottles with those swing wire-and-ceramic tops. My favourite was dandelion and burdock. I've since wondered if the spread of the coronavirus had any effect on the company's sales. Incidentally, who'd have thought that dandelion and burdock was first created by St Thomas Aquinas? Nobody, as it turns out – it's not true. One of those urban myths.

- Ginger beer and lime: I was introduced to the pleasures of this drink (I suppose that today you'd call it a mocktail) when I was around thirteen, after a golf tournament in Morfa Nefyn. Golf-wise the tournament was a disaster (I lost all my balls, and no, that's not a metaphor), but drinks-wise it was a revelation, and I imbibed little else until I was introduced to the pleasures of alcohol. I've not tasted it since – I really must try it again, though it'll be with trepidation: I don't think I could bear the disappointment if it's really rubbish. My daughter has since informed me that it's a Moscow Mule without the alcohol. Though how she would know that I've no idea.

- Orangina: not a blast from my *own* past exactly, but from that of my children. During the 1980s, whenever we toured France in our caravan, one of the highlights for the kids was being able to drink orangina – you couldn't get it in the UK. Now you can – I tried it last week. Same bottle, same taste. It was actually delicious, but the availability of everything, everywhere, does rub some of the bloom off international travel.

The only other non-alcoholic drink I can remember enjoying was milk. I think it must have been fashionable in the early Sixties among us teenage trendsetters. Or perhaps the wider use of fridges meant that milk was at last palatable – cold milk I still find delicious, milk at room temperature is revolting. I often ordered milk in Brexo, and it was a penny cheaper if you asked in Welsh – the owner was a fierce nationalist, one of the Tryweryn bombers. How south Walians got on I don't know – in north Wales 'milk' is *llefrith*, understood by all. In south Wales it was *'llaeth'*, which in the north meant 'buttermilk'. I don't think Brexo served buttermilk.

Childhood drinks – postscript

A number of comments arose from the post:

- It was generally agreed that there was a stretch of road between Y Ffôr and Llanaelhaearn known as Vimto Valley, but there was disagreement about the reason for that name. Either:
  - o There was a billboard advertising Vimto at the start of that stretch, or
  - o A Vimto delivery lorry had, at some time in the past, crashed there.

- The owners of Vimto had a holiday cottage (boo!) behind the Vaynol in Abersoch. This has not been confirmed.

- My daughter informed me that 'Cheeky Vimto' is so-called not only because it's a similar colour to Vimto, but also because it actually tastes like it. This remains to be checked out. By me.

- I was advised by my brother that, if I think Lucozade is the same colour as urine, I should see a doctor.

- My brother also reminded me that, when he was a kid and demanding some pop of a particular flavour, I told him that there was no difference in taste from one flavour to another. I challenged him to a blind tasting. He was disgruntled to discover that I was right.

- My daughter then added that I'd done the same to her, but with fruit gums.

- This is, in fact, an example of how knowledge can be passed down through the generations. In the 1950s I'd gone to Steven Morgan's birthday party in his flat above W H Smiths, and an argument had broken out about which was the best flavour of Corona. Mr Morgan claimed that there was no difference and, yes, challenged us to a blind tasting. And yes, he was right. A lesson I've clearly never forgotten.

- I've since drunk 'cheeky Vimto', courtesy of my daughter and son-in-law. Yes, it does taste like Vimto. And, unlike Vimto, it can get you very very drunk.

Teenage drinks

Writing about childhood drinks in my last post led me, inevitably, to alcoholic drinks during adolescence.

In many respects, the whole attitude to alcohol in Pwllheli was complicated:

- First there was class:
  o The working-class drank in pubs, or in the British Legion.
  o The middle-class drank at home, in each other's houses, or at the golf club.
  o The upper-class – who knew? There seemed to be no nobs around. Presumably they drank in their ancestral piles, but nobody saw them. If indeed they existed at all in our neck of the woods.
- Then there was age:
  o Grown-ups drank at home, in pubs, in clubs, in hotels, and in church during communion.
  o Teenagers drank at the side of the harbour, in the shelters on the prom, behind the church hall during youth club, on the children's playground in Ffordd y Maer, on the dunes in South Beach and in places too numerous to mention around the Garn. Also, possibly at home if their parents were out, or even better, if they were away.
- Then there was politics, though this I find hard to talk about with any authority. In my memory, the only real political club in Pwllheli was the Conservative Club. Yet it seemed that Tories were, in Pwllheli, an endangered species – everybody was Plaid or Labour. They all used the Con Club, though. The Liberal Club, as far as I remember, didn't have a bar.

- Then there was religion. Again, I find it hard to talk about this. Methodists, I knew, were by and large anti-booze. Otherwise it was every man/woman for him/her self.

Anyway, that's the context. Let's now get down to the nitty-gritty. What did we actually drink?

Alcoholic drinks in my mid-teens were initially confined to:

- Cider (which adults, bless them, seemed to think was suitable for kids, presumably in the mistaken belief that it contained no, or very little, alcohol. It was in fact stronger than beer.). When I was fifteen I got very much the worse for wear on cider in Blackpool. I've never drunk it since. Though I have been back to Blackpool.

- British sherry, the booze of choice of the mid-teens because:
  o It could be obtained from any off-licence that wasn't too fussy about age-restrictions.
  o It was strong enough to uncork your innermost secrets – even who you fancied. Though you'd deny it the next day.

- Alcopops lay in the future, and played no part in my adolescence.

At home (or my home, anyway) adults drank whisky and soda or gin and tonic (men) and gin and It, port and lemon, Babycham or Cherry B (women). And not very much else, or indeed, not very much at all.

In our initial forays into pubs (from the age of fifteen onwards), a whole new world of drinks was introduced:

- Mild. I once asked for a pint of mild in a London pub. The Aussie barman looked blank and appealed for help from his supervisor, who explained 'It's a regional beer, drunk mainly in the north.' That put me in my place.

- Draught bitter. Which I would swig, hold the glass out in front of me, shake my head in awed admiration and say, 'Great pint.' Then, trying not to throw up, I'd cram crisps into my mouth to take away the taste. I seem to remember Tom Jones owning up to similar shenanigans when he was a lad.

- Various keg beers started to creep in – Red Barrel and Worthington E for example (on draught, in pubs). Also the canned beers like Party Fours and Party Sevens. They could get you pissed, sure, but they weren't particularly nice. And if you didn't have the special tool, with triangular blade, you were jiggered.

- Mixed. Half of mild, half of bitter. Mixed. Hence the name. Never took to it myself.

- Brown mixed (also known, in other parts of the UK, as brown topper, brown cobber, brown split and many others). It was not very strong (though it was dark and looked manly), quite sweet, and acceptable to a novice palate. If the landlord poured the brown ale in first and topped it with mild from the pump, you'd never go to that pub again. When it was done the other way around, you always ended up with more than a half of mild in your glass, and therefore more than a pint when you added the brown. This was a good thing, and made you want to return. Pouring the brown ale into the half of bitter in the pint glass was an art – done properly, the ale clugged into the glass while, simultaneously, the foam flowed up into the bottle. Which, after settling, you could add to your glass later. Brown mixed was my drink of choice into adulthood.

- Black and tan: Guinness and cider (originally, apparently, guinness and champagne, but how many teenagers could afford champagne?).

- Snakebite: lager and cider, sometimes with a dash of blackcurrant.

- Rum and black: popular with lads who'd joined the Merchant Navy.

Beyond this, I can't really remember. My children and grandchildren seem to imbibe either real ales (which weren't really a thing back then, except for Worthington White Shield) or a wide (and wild) variety of cocktails (also not a thing back then).

The dangers of alcohol are clear for all to see. It can disrupt families, destroy lives. Somebody once said that alcohol is a good friend but a bad mistress.

All I can say is that, without it, I don't think I could have survived growing up. Or adulthood. Or old age! Though of course, in the end, nobody survives old age.

So. Cheers!

Teenage drinks – postscript

The response to the post on teenage drinks demonstated the importance of accuracy, the imperative of doing conscientious research and steering clear of things you know nothing about. Never having actually drunk a black and tan, I confused it with black velvet. Which I've also never drunk.

- Black and tan was a cocktail of stout and pale ale – you could see the dark Guinness lying on top of the tan IPA. Its history goes back to eighteenth-century London taverns, where landlords would mix heavily-taxed strong ale with other weaker, and therefore cheaper, beers. Incidentally, never order a 'black and tan' in Ireland – that was the nickname of a much hated reserve force recruited (often from ex-soldiers) to reinforce the British during the War of Independence. Ask instead for a pint of 'half and half'.

- It was black velvet that was a mixture of Guinness and either cider or sparkling wine.

Apologies to all who were forced to correct me. As a penance, I'm off to the pub to do the research I should have done before: to drink a pint of black and tan, then a pint of black velvet. Probably to be followed by chasers of rum and black and cheeky vimto. I draw the line at cider, snakebite, or especially cider with rum and black tipped in. I don't want to vomit, or (see next section) to look like a clown in the morning.

Other responses included:

- From someone who should know, the founding of Pwllheli's Conservative Club, and its subsequent popularity, had nothing to do with politics and everything to do with the Sunday closing of pubs (that is, the Lord's Day absence of alternatives) and the highly competitive prices at the pumps or the optics. Well, that's a relief!

- Underage drinking by young women at the Penlan Fawr was rife, despite Mrs Blake's best efforts. It also went on at the Tŷ Coch in Morfa Nefyn, the Ship in Edern and the Tu Hwnt i'r Afon in Rhyd-y-clafdy. I can't corroborate this – I'm neither young nor a woman. My brother Jeff, who had a summer job as a Crossville bus conductor, told me that, when his bus stopped at the top end of Llanbedrog, he would see young women, who'd bought a half-price ticket on the bus, go into the Ship for a drink. In a matter of seconds they'd aged five years, from thirteen to eighteen. A good example, perhaps, of Einstein's theory of the relativity of time.

- The underage *serving* of drinks was not unknown either. A (then seventeen-year-old) member of the group attested to the good influences of working as a waiter in Butlins' Pig and Whistle, both on his knowledge of cocktails and his mental arithmetic. Whether or not it affected his moral compass, I couldn't say.

- Bangor University students apparently enjoyed rum and blacks poured into pints of cider. The effects of this horrendous witches brew were not recorded, but the 'wonderful wide red smile' it gave them the next morning meant there was little point in claiming that not a drop had passed their lips. It must also have made them look really happy when they really really weren't.

- A member of the group (yes, my friend Tony Pierce), long resident in France and on a business trip to London, found himself in a Soho tavern confused by the array of lager and keg taps and the absence of the traditional pump handles he remembered from his youth. He tried to order real ale, to the confusion of the Romanian barmaid, and had to settle for a keg beer which didn't impress him much. When asked by me what manner of business took him to Soho, he claimed that he was 'just taking a short cut.' To the nearest Non-conformist chapel, presumably. To pray.

- A comprehensive comment introduced the perspective of somebody who had had to put up with extreme chapel disapproval of alcohol. He also provided a detailed addendum on the social effects. I'll quote it (with his permission) in full:

> A very interesting take on booze and boozing!
> But my word, what you townies got up to...! The
> Temperance movement which led to millions
> pledging never to let a drop of alcohol pass their lips
> was still alive and well in rural Llŷn. The teetotalism
> was also responsible for the pubs still being closed
> on Sundays. It survived until 1996, which was why
> all the clubs thrived! From Conservative to Golf,
> British Legion to Toc H, they did a roaring trade.
> Meanwhile, many villages like Morfa Nefyn and
> Pentrefelin no longer had pubs, because they had
> been closed down by said Bible-punching puritans
> in the nineteenth and early twentieth century.
> However, the sea-faring towns and villages of Nefyn,
> Aberdaron, Edern, Tudweiliog and Pwllheli were
> made of sterner stuff, and resisted the pressure of
> the chapels.

One can tell you never had to sit through a real tirade of a chapel preacher in full temperance mode! Hell and damnation were to be our lot if we dared touch the demon drink...! And as for the social/class differences... Pubs were generally the domain of men, so the only women were barmaids. Women still wore gloves and hat to go out and generally never entered a pub, or never alone and usually only on the arm of an escort who always paid. If she entered at all, because nice girls did not! Lounge bars were added to encourage the ladies post war. This was also why social drinking was usually done at home or in clubs. As for the upper-class... Same here as elsewhere and up to the present. Their own homes or as house guests in the country/up in town/abroad, clubs, board rooms, theatres and hotels.

All true, so let's hear it for seafaring Nefyn, Aberdaron, Edern, Tudweiliog and Pwllheli! Bulwarks against fundamentalist booze-bashing!

CHAPTER 2

Places we went

IF MEMORIES OF our upbringing are made up mainly of things we did, they have to include the places that we did them in.

Studt's fairground

Studt's fairground was an ever-present part of '50s and '60s Pwllheli. I've got a vague memory of it initially being a travelling fair which visited the town only periodically – twice a year, I think – with the most important being *Ffair Pen Tymor*, the annual agricultural hiring fair. But for most of my childhood and youth it was a permanent fixture. Its position – near the slaughterhouse and the sewage pipe that crossed that part of the harbour – doesn't sound very enticing, but to my childhood self it was magical. My adolescent self, though, had mixed feelings.

Now, over sixty years later, it's hard to separate what I actually recall from what I've since picked up in other fairgrounds. Was there a ghost-train or not – I can't remember. I'm sure there wasn't a helter-skelter. Or was there? But certainly, the heart of Studt's fairground was the 'dodgems' (the name reflecting how they were supposed to be driven) or 'bumping cars' (which more accurately reflected the reality). They offered us kids our first taste of driving. It wasn't very realistic – you could reverse only by turning the steering-wheel full lock, and you could cheerfully crash into as many other cars as you liked without any serious medical or legal consequences. But hey, it had a steering wheel and a foot pedal, and you were in charge!

Next to the dodgems stood the walzters – round spinning cars fixed to a rotating and undulating track that revolved around a central kiosk. People paid to go on the waltzers. I'd have happily paid not to.

Around these two main attractions were stalls – coconut shy, hook-a-duck, roll-a-penny, hoop-la, ping-pong balls aimed at massed goldfish bowls – together with a penny-arcade and a row of boat-swings. The whole experience was topped with an overlay of deafening noise – of collisions, the screams they provoked and the crackling flashes and sparks from the pole-mounted pick-ups above the dodgems, of the terrified shrieks of people being tortured by the G-forces of the waltzers, of the clattering of ball-bearings and the ringing of bells from the penny-arcade, of the shouted come-ons of the stall-minders, of the roar of the generators and the blast of rock music being pumped out at ear-splitting volume all over the site and, indeed, the town.

The smells too bring back vibrant memories – of candy floss, toffee apples, fried onions, burgers and hot dogs, and the sharp electric smell of the dodgems. As a child the whole experience was vividly exciting – moving from ride to ride, stall to stall, exulting over the winning of soft toys or goldfish in plastic bags, munching on food that would end up making you queasy. Sensory overload as a substitute for alcohol or mind-altering drugs!

Adolescence injected a destabilising sexual ingredient into this heady brew. The fair provided ample opportunities for us teenage lads to compete with each other and, more importantly, show off our imagined skill, strength and courage to the girls. The battleground was the punchbag machine, the high striker/strength tester with its huge mallet, the shooting gallery, the coconut shy. We could prove our bravery and skill on the dodgems (though in my case at least, certainly not on the waltzers).

Competition among your mates was one thing, but there was a darker side to the whole experience. In particular, I found the lads who worked on the rides intimidating. They invariably looked tough and fit, with tight jeans and shirt-sleeves rolled up above bulging biceps. They jumped onto the back of dodgems to take the fares from the boys while flirting with their girlfriends, or swung onto waltzers where an expert twirl would trigger hysterical female screaming. I really hated those lads. How could my main strength – getting good marks in school – compete!

Since then, returning to my home town with wife and children introduced me to some of the simpler pleasures of parenthood. My kids could, as I did, play the machines in the penny-arcade or try to win goldfish or soft toys in the booths. As an added bonus, they were easier to impress with my prowess on the dodgems, and were more likely to forgive my lack of it in the shooting gallery or the coconut shy than were my mates or the girls we were with. It was like returning to the safety of my own childhood while vaulting over the painful inadequacy of my adolescence.

I now realise that the Studt's were a well-known and highly respected fairground family, whose seven generations went back to at least 1837. Their fame reached beyond Wales. When I lived in Yorkshire, our neighbour was from a travelling fairground family, and he immediately recognised the Studt name. Pwllheli, as a place to grow up in and as a holiday destination for outsiders, owes a debt of gratitude to the family. Looking back from the vantage point of my seventies, I can appreciate the vivid, vibrant otherness that the Studt's fairground injected into my life.

But I still really *really* hate the guys who worked on the rides.

Studt's fairground – postscript

The enduring memories of Studt's fairground seem to have been happy ones for most of our Facebook group – of childhood visits in the '50s and '60s, or of taking our own children in later years. But the effects of ageing were apparent – while the remembered deafening music that could be heard throughout the town seems to have been generally approved-of during adolescence, in old age we felt that today it would have been totally unacceptable. I pitied the poor people living close to the fairground – how on earth did they survive?

One specific memory was met with universal horror – the 'Sooty and Sweep Show' in the arcade, which belted out 'The Grand Old Duke of York'. It was a coin-operated machine which played the song on a loop. One commentator added a link to a YouTube clip of the actual machine, leading to a flurry of negative comments – 'I can still hear the bloody thing!'

Oh, and yes, there *was* a ghost-train.

Over the river

Although we kids could play anywhere in Pwllheli that took our fancy, there were certain defined areas to which we tended to return, depending on what particular games we had in mind. The town centre was varied. Shops in which to irritate the assistants and, on occasion, slip stuff surreptitiously into our pockets and walk quickly out. Streets in which to peer through the windows of parked cars to note the top speeds on their speedometers, fondly imagining that they could actually achieve those speeds. Hidey-holes in which to sit, smoke, and observe the passing scene – above the post box at the bottom of Salem Terrace, for example, watching the clouds of butterflies attracted by its large and unruly buddleia bush growing out of the wall.

And there were loads of places to just hang around in – Studt's funfair (loud and raucous), Gimblet Rock (invigorating when stormy), the dunes on South Beach (calm and lovely in summer), the shelters on the prom (smelly, but at least out of the wind) the harbour (good for fishing off, or underage drinking beside), the Garn (a huge natural adventure playground), the swings in Ffordd-y-Maer (thronged with kids and their mums during the day, teenagers at night).

But (and finally to get to the point) one of our favourite places was 'over the river'. The river was (according to Google maps, which I've just checked) Afon Dwyryd. I'm sure *we* called it 'Afon Goch' – Red River. Why we called it that I've no idea – perhaps because there was a popular song at the time – 'Red River Rock'. Or perhaps we imagined it running red with the blood of our enemies. There was certainly something militaristic about our attitude to it.

It was on the opposite side of the Garn from the town. To get there, we'd march up Llŷn Street, then at the top of the hill, just as it starts to slope down towards Efailnewydd, wheel right through the kissing gate, pass the ruined 'Old Barns', then drop down to the river itself. In those days the path was shaded by a hazel grove, its trees heavy with nuts in the autumn. I don't know if they're still there. The trees that is, not the nuts.

The woodland on the opposite bank was our target – our main hunting ground. Sometimes for snakes (I once saw a grass snake at least a yard long writhe across a sunlit clearing), occasionally for birds' nests, but mainly for sticks. Either general purpose sticks for thrashing aside nettles, vaulting over rivulets, or indulging in combat like Robin Hood and Little John. Or ones for making bows and arrows and taflars (catapults). And over the river wasn't just good for sticks, bows, arrows and catapults. It was terrific for building dens. Even warriors needed shelter.

But first we had to cross the river, and this required military engineering savvy of a high order. And not sticks, but substantial poles. Two of them. These had to be suspended from trees on either side of the river – one at foot height, the other, slightly offset, at shoulder height. These allowed you to shuffle sideways on the bottom pole while holding onto the top one.

Cutting the poles would have been no problem if we'd carried heavy duty saws or axes. But we didn't. So it required relays of us, with much prized but rather small pocket knives, to cut down two saplings, then strip them of branches and leaves. The bad thing was that this took absolutely ages. The good thing was that, once built, the crossing could be used for weeks or months. Just like the bridges built by the Royal Engineers on any battlefield you'd care to name. Or even the Romans, millennia ago.

But to get back to Afon Goch, and Red River Rock. Johnny and the Hurricanes released their single in 1959. We kids were, at that time, between thirteen and fifteen years old, so right at the very end of our childhood and at the very start of our adolescence. Soon, the explosion of the Sixties, the delights of Brexo and its jukebox, the dances at the Legion, the films at the Town Hall or the Palladium, the attractions of the opposite sex, would engulf us, and shoe-horn us into the adult world. Perhaps 'Red River Rock' symbolises for me the passage from childhood to adolescence.

That said, 'over the river' was a lovely place to be. Mossy, dotted with drifts of bluebells and primroses, full of birdsong, lit by sunlight angled down through the overhead canopy.

And during childhood the weather was *always* sunny – haven't you noticed?

Over the river – postscript
The post led to three principal threads in the comments:
- The main response was discussion of
  o why the river was called 'Afon Goch';
  o where it rose;
  o where it had been before arriving 'over the river';
  o and where it subsequently went.
- All this involved a level of knowledge of the area that was

way beyond me. Perhaps other kids ranged more widely than I and my friends did, or perhaps this knowledge was attained afterwards, during a period of adulthood long after I'd left Pwllheli.

- There was also a belated thanks – sixty years after the fact – for the pole bridges we built. The respondent had used them himself without having any idea who put them there. A bit like the people of the Dark Ages and Roman roads.

- I was taken to task for not mentioning 'Three Founders Cave', a derelict lead mine. That knocked on the head a future post that I was planning to write.

Cei

Not many people in today's Pwllheli are old enough to remember 'Cei'. It was a ruined jumble of masonry, weeds and threadbare grass in the angle between the bottom of Penlan Street and Mitre Place. I thought at the time that it was a bomb site, and we played there quite a lot when I was little, just as kids of all ages played on bomb sites across the country – Liverpool, Manchester, London – indeed any conurbation that had been blitzed during the war. Perhaps that's why I assumed it was a bomb site – I'd seen so many of them on Pathé Pictorials at the cinema, swarming with children making dens out of sheets of corrugated iron or smashing windows in derelict buildings.

Since then, I've started to wonder. Surely Pwllheli was too small to have been a worthwhile target for the Luftwaffe? Perhaps a rogue bomber jettisoning its payload as it fled home, having been seen off over Liverpool by the RAF? Or less romantically, perhaps just a ruined building gutted by a domestic fire? When I Googled 'Cei', it came up with 'Hotel Cei Bach', '0.2 miles from Pwllheli's city centre'. Not much help there! And 'city centre'?!

I can pin down fairly accurately when we used to play in

Cei. It must have been after the start of the 1950s. Before that, I would have been too young to be allowed out on my own. Later (in or after 1953, presumably) Cei was developed into the Coronation Gardens, and so became too well-ordered to provide a bolt-hole for kids. But during that magical two-or-three-year period, on winter evenings, away from adults' prying eyes, we could clamber around its broken stonework, light fires, play hide-and-seek, tell ghost stories, play 'Kiss or kill' or 'Truth, dare, command or promise', lit only by the lampposts of the surrounding streets.

Then the forces of progress (or 'the Council' as they've since become known) came along to celebrate the accession of Queen Elizabeth II, tidied up the masonry, laid down lawns and planted flower beds. I hope her majesty appreciated it. We kids, like the cowboys and plains Indians of the American West, were forced out, to live our lives elsewhere: around the harbour, on the Garn or Gimblet Rock, or along the dunes of South Beach and West End. Free spirits constrained only, and alas, by the march of civilization. The final coup de grâce came when the Coronation Gardens in their turn were replaced by the shops at the bottom of Penlan Street and down towards the Maes. Free spirits finally ousted by commerce.

I wondered if any other members of the group knew about this unsung and unofficial adventure playground? I looked up the word 'Cei' in my Welsh dictionary, and it means simply 'Quay'. So was it the site of Pwllheli's quayside before the harbour was built? Was it a bomb site, as we kids imagined? Or just a scruffy undeveloped corner of the town, forgotten for a while, then brought into the mainstream?

Cei – postscript

Several interesting snippets of information arose from the comments:

- It was thought that 'Cei' *was* indeed the site of the Customs House, handily positioned on what was then the quayside. But this was way back in the mid-nineteenth century, so not prompted by the memory of even the oldest inhabitants!

- It was also the site of a tannery owned by William Lloyd Ellis, who ran a leather shop across the road on the corner of Station Square. This comment sparked a vague memory of my own – the smell of leather in what later became the Tourist Office.
- It was, somebody else recalled, the site of one of the town's Guy Fawkes night bonfires, though that stopped when it became the Coronation Gardens.
- Cei was later bought by the father of one of our group members, who briefly ran a crazy golf course on it.
- Tony Pierce, who later became a mate of mine, used to break into the Co-op storage yard on the other side of Penlan Street to drink illicit cider while keeping a weather-eye open for the watchman. I'm glad we later became friends – my good example probably saved him from a life of crime.

Half-remembered places

I can recall most of the places in and around Pwllheli that we kicked around in very clearly – not only the places themselves, but how they related to each other. I could arrive in the centre of the town today and walk, slowly but unerringly, to each one. But I have several memories that are indistinct and seem to lack any sort of context. I have no real idea where they were and wouldn't be able to find them now to save my life.

For example, I recall climbing, with friends, up from Abererch Road into the hills between it and Caernarfon Road. I have general memories of great views of Cardigan Bay opening up as we climbed, of gorse bushes festooned in spiders' webs, and of the spiders themselves – plump, with colourful markings (yellow? black? white?) in a cross on their backs. Poison spiders, we warned one another earnestly, and gave them a wide berth.

Of specific memories, though, I have only two:

- A reservoir. It looked a bit like a swimming pool, but with no ladders or lines on the bottom.

- An aeroplane. We broke out of the bushes onto a tidily-mown field in front of a large house, and there before us stood a light aircraft. We could see that it had a framework (wood? metal? I don't know) covered in yellow treated canvas. What intrigued us was that on one of the wings, this covering sported a large zip.

Having spent most of my life wondering about these half-memories, it suddenly occurred to me that, with the might of the internet and the World Wide Web packed into my mobile phone, I need wonder no longer. I fetched up Google Earth, zoomed in on Pwllheli, and set to:

- Surely the reservoir would be easy to spot. Not at all – no trace.

- The plane would of course be long gone. But without doubt I'd be able to find the big house. Again, nothing.

My other half-memory was of a footpath which started on Llŷn Street (where it began to slope down towards Efailnewydd) and ended up, after meandering through a farm, somewhere on the road to Nefyn. Again, I remember only two things:

- What we called a windmill – one of those wind pumps you see scattered across the outback in Australia and the American Midwest, looking like an electricity pylon but with a circle of sails and a rudder to keep them facing into the wind. We clambered around on it, and even enjoyed rather dangerous games of three-dimensional tick.

- At the end of the footpath we came down to the Nefyn road, near a sort of pull-off where there used to be heavy equipment and piles of gravel, presumably for highway repair.

Again, modern technology let me down. I found what might have been the path – to and from a farm – but there was no way of knowing if it was the right one, and I certainly could find no trace of the windmill. Probably long dismantled.

Yet it seemed unlikely that a reservoir nestling high in the hills above Pwllheli, that a house in roughly the same area which boasted a private airstrip, that a farm owning its own wind pump lying somewhere at the top of Llŷn Street, would be entirely forgotten.

If any of my co-survivors from those far-off days could rummage about in the attics of their minds and help me out, I'd be very grateful.

Half-remembered places – postscript

I can't believe that these half-remembered places – the reservoir, the house with a plane standing on its landing-strip, the outback-style wind pump – had festered deep in my unconscious for over half a century, when all I had to do was bring them up on Facebook and all would be revealed!

First the reservoir. I immediately found out what it was called (Nant Stigallt Reservoir, called by many Ffynnon Fawr) and where it is (overlooking Pwllheli Marina), but there was some disagreement over its purpose ('Surely it was too small to provide Pwllheli's needs,' said one group member, provoking from another the scurrilous suggestion that people in Pwllheli didn't wash very often, so didn't need much water).

My feeling that it was rather small was echoed by others ('I've seen bigger private swimming pools in people's gardens'). The possible source of its water completely foxed me. Mur Quimp was suggested, but when I Googled the name, arrived only at an Airbnb near Llanbedrog.

Then the aeroplane. It was quickly agreed that what we kids had stumbled upon was part of the Broom Hall estate. This set me off on an orgy of research that established that:

- Broom Hall estate had a private airstrip. The heir to the estate was a flying enthusiast who was killed in April 1937 when his plane hit a wall.

- In 1946 Billy Butlin, in the process of converting HMS Glendower into Butlins Pwllheli, bought the estate in order to run pleasure flights from the airstrip. He proceeded to buy more land nearby to expand the strip.

- Two small aviation companies, Cambrian Airways and Dragon Airways, ran flights from Broom Hall, to, respectively, Cardiff and Dublin.

- At some point the airstrip was used by Pwllheli and District Gliding Club.

- Flights stopped in the '60s and the extra land, upon which today sheep peacefully graze, was sold back to the original owners.

- I looked up the several types of aircraft mentioned and concluded that the one we'd seen was an Auster.

The whole topic certainly introduced me to the pre- and post-Second World War free-for-all that was commercial aviation.

Finally, the Australian Outback wind pump was pinpointed as to location (in Penmaen Fields, near Ffynnon Felin Fach), and was photographed as it now is, looking exactly as it did then (but without its sails).

A bonus was a little brief history of the tiny yard on the road to Nefyn – at different times a builder's yard, a storage area for static caravans, even a travellers' encampment.

Isn't it amazing that a scant handful of misty half-remembered recollections can lead to concrete suggestions from locals who know the area which in turn point the way to further research?

Thanks to all who chipped in!

Hospitals

Throughout adulthood, being one of life's pessimists, whenever I've been buying a house I've tried to make sure that it's close to a hospital. And as I've got older, proximity to a hospital has climbed from the 'if possible' list, through 'highly desirable' to the top of 'essential'. I think this obsession has got worse the closer I get to meeting my maker. But it might also be traced back to when I broke my leg playing rugby when I was in the sixth form. More of which in a minute.

Growing up in our part of north Wales, I was always vaguely aware that there were three commonly used hospitals in the region. Working outwards from Pwllheli, they were:

- Cartref – in Pwllheli itself.

- Bryn Beryl, about three miles out on the road to Caernarfon.

- C&A in Bangor, the nearest general hospital, and about thirty miles away.

A fourth, Gobowen, I came across only once. My brother Jeff, on his way to Bangor after plummeting from a gasometer in Pwllheli, fell (oh please!) into conversation with an old lady in the back of the ambulance. She warned him against all local hospitals and advised him to go to Gobowen, near Oswestry. When he asked why, she told him that she had been unnecessarily opened up at the main hospital in Bangor. She described it graphically – 'O'm gwddw i'm twll' ('from my throat to my hole').

He had some difficulty not laughing, and in persuading her not to show him the scar.

As I mentioned, my own first experience of hospital was when I broke my leg playing rugby, so I'll start with that.

Caernarfonshire & Anglesey Hospital

It was my own fault, really – down to youthful exuberance, allied to total incompetence. If you're not interested in the technicalities of rugby, skip the next bit.

It was a home game against HMS Conway, on our West End pitch just behind the beach. I was playing scrum half. I'd received the ball from the forwards in the lineout and had elected to kick for touch. In training, Harry Hughes had impressed upon us in no uncertain terms that if you kicked for touch and failed to find it, it was your bounden duty to the rest of the team to sprint upfield in order to put them on-side.

I missed touch and, following Harry's instructions, sprinted upfield. Meanwhile, the defending full back had fielded the ball competently and himself kicked for touch. Successfully. He put on the brakes, sliding forward, boots first, body leaning backwards. Having seen that he'd done so, I put on the brakes, sliding forward, boots first, body leaning backwards. My left leg went under him, the rest of me went over him. There was a sound like a rifle-shot.

The HMS Conway trainer bustled up, confidently announced that the leg wasn't broken, and allowed my team-mates to lift me up. The leg immediately sagged at an alarming angle. Both tibia and fibula, had snapped cleanly half-way between knee and ankle. He hurriedly told them to put me back down.

I was carried off the pitch on a gate lifted off its hinges in a nearby field. I felt like, and must have looked like, Cleopatra.

Waiting for the ambulance on Cardiff Road, my GP, doctor Gwenda, gave me an injection which did a lot more than stop the pain. By the time the ambulance finally arrived, I was not only pain-free, I think I might even have been singing! I was spirited away, with Harry Hughes and my father in attendance.

On the way to Bangor, Harry and my father chatted companionably. Harry told a joke. A queue of people, knocking on the gates of heaven, respond in turn to St Peter's 'Who's there?' with, 'It's me.' This went on for some time. Finally, when another hopeful answers, 'It is I,' St Peter turns to God and sniggers. 'Another bloody English teacher!'

I laughed excessively. Partly because teachers didn't normally swear. Partly because it wasn't a bad joke. Nothing at all to do with the medication.

When I got to C&A, still in my rugby kit, my leg was X-rayed (by a young, sympathetic and extremely pretty girl who seemed not much older than myself), then swathed in plaster by a burly male nurse.

That night, in bed in my attic room in Llŷn Street, I thought about the day's experiences, and decided that I was mightily impressed with a hospital which hadn't always had the best of reviews.

After returning to C&A some weeks later to have the cast adapted for walking, I had reason to reconsider.

In the waiting room, as I sat in a wheelchair with my leg sticking out ahead of me on a plank, a nurse sideswiped the cast with her hip as she bustled past, sending it, and my leg, crashing to the floor. I yelled out in pain. Far from apologising, she glared at me as if to say that it was a stupid place to leave a leg, especially one heavily plastered from toe to crotch, and stalked righteously off.

Later, stretched out on a hospital trolley after having had a plaster-soaked sponge lashed onto the foot of my cast, I was wheeled into a small side room and forgotten. I was there for hours. The room was stifling, sweat poured off me, but nobody came. Finally, fearing death by dehydration, I worked my way along the wall with my hands, got myself and the trolley over to the door, swung it open and shouted weakly for help. It came in the form of an orderly who, when I told him what had happened, looked extremely embarrassed. He made sure I got on the next ambulance back to Pwllheli.

That night, lying in my bed (now moved downstairs to the front room) in Llŷn Street, I thought over the day. Perhaps my brother's elderly ambulance friend had been right.

During my final visit to C&A, the plaster cast was removed (terrifyingly with a circular saw and a pair of giant shears) and replaced with sheets of Elastoplast off a huge roll. Not too bad, but with consequences which I'll come to in the next post.

This one's getting too long. On, in the next one, to Cartref and Bryn Beryl.

C&A – postscript

Since the Caernarfonshire and Anglesey Hospital in Bangor served the whole of those two counties, it's not surprising that my memory of attending for treatment stirred up those of many others. In no particular order:

- Two siblings in the children's ward for the removal of both tonsils and adenoids. A fraught experience.

- A tearful little boy begging his parents to take him home and bring him back after his sixth birthday. 'I'll be much braver by then.'

- A story from a close friend who'd been rushed to C&A after a car accident on the road back from the Glyn-y-Weddw to Pwllheli. (Note for those who don't know the area – the Glyn-y-Weddw is a pub. Draw your own conclusions.) A big deal, and I'd never heard about it before!

- A girl who'd been hospitalised four times with broken arms – the last time when thrown while riding a bullock. They breed them tough on Llŷn!

- I was reprimanded for leaving out two other hospitals, in Bangor and Caernarfon. I'd never attended, or even heard of, either. So apologies, but these are *my* memories!

- The horrible effects of taking off plaster casts were dealt with in detail. The foul smell, the dead skin, the wasted muscles. When I had the cast removed, I'd blithely said that I'd hitch-hike home from Bangor. What an idiot! Any sudden movement of my leg caused agony, and I was still on crutches two weeks later.

- And finally, I loved the fact that, after all these years, the post led to a lightbulb moment for one member of the group who'd always thought that 'C&A' stood for 'Children and Adults'. Bless!

Cartref

Further to my round-up of local hospitals in north Wales.

Cartref, in Pwllheli, was based in the old workhouse building on Ala Road. Only two memories spring to mind:

- In my first year in the sixth form (or Form Six as we called it), I had to have a huge sheet of Elastoplast removed from my lower leg, applied after the removal of a groin-to-toe plaster-cast in C&A (see last post). The physiotherapist in Cartref clipped through the dressing, then without warning ripped it off, dead yellow flaking skin, leg hair and all. I'd like to report that I bore the pain with stoicism, my only reaction being a tightening of my jaw muscles and a slight widening of my eyes. I'd like to, but I can't. I screamed at the top of my voice. The other guys in the unit paled and turned to the wall. She then asked me to squat and lift myself up on the poorly leg. I told her that I couldn't do that on my healthy leg, never mind one that had been in a cast for three months. Her distain was palpable. But I didn't take it personally – she was clearly a psychopath.

- As 'A' Levels approached, I fainted several times at home. I was referred to Cartref. I'm not sure what they thought was wrong, but they weighed me, measured my height, and tested my eyesight. Clearly the eyes had it. After the application of drops, I was returned to the waiting room. I took a magazine off the table and started to leaf through it. I couldn't focus. I tried holding it further and further away. To no avail. I felt sure that there was nothing wrong with my eyes (you tend to be very sure of your opinions at that age). It was obvious that the problem was that my arms weren't long enough. When the doctor returned, I was standing on a chair with the magazine on the floor. He handed me down and announced that my eyesight wasn't the trouble. No surprise there, then. I never thought it was. He further offered the opinion (still in the waiting room, patient confidentiality clearly not being an issue in those days) it was probably to do with my age – that I'd outgrown my strength. I accepted this gracefully. Though, in the spirit of scientific observation, I'd have to add that, looking back, whenever I fainted it was either after a long night's revision, or a heavy evening out with the boys.

Fainting fits have never bothered me since, except occasionally after a heavy night out. With the boys or otherwise.

Cartref – postscript
A mixed bag of comments:

- The tearing off of the leg elastoplast provoked the facetious comment, 'Reminds me of my first Brazilian'.

- At Cartref, one unfortunate was treated for 'fallen arches' by having his feet stuck into a bowl of water through which an electric current was then passed. He failed to tell us whether this resulted in his arches rising.

- When Cartref was the town workhouse, several characters who'd lived there were mentioned. Bob I remember – the clue was in his nickname (Bob Workhouse). But I hadn't realised that Pyrs Matches was an inmate as well. He was employed as 'muscle' for John Goddards (not in the gangster sense, but in the furniture removal sense), and, allegedly, had started to take his clothes off in preparation for a swim when, driving through the Mersey Tunnel, he was told that they were under the river.

- Another comment not only painted an irresistible picture,

but widened my vocabulary. Apparently, local bobbies, when doing their rounds, used to duck into Cartref to be fed coffee and luncheon-meat sandwiches by the kitchen staff, and while there would report inaccurate 'locstats' by phone to the police station, a hundred yards away. No, I didn't know what it meant either – Location Status. So while living high on the hog in Cartref's kitchen, they would be credited with pounding the beat far and wide elsewhere in the town.

Bryn Beryl

I've posted recently about local hospitals in my part of north Wales. C&A in Bangor, Cartref in Pwllheli, I experienced both when I was a kid, Bryn Beryl, though, is more part of my mother's dotage than my childhood.

Apart from driving past it, three miles after starting off from Pwllheli, on my way back to England, my only experience of Bryn Beryl came through Mum.

Towards the end of her life, she was always worried about going into hospital. Whenever she was referred to Bryn Beryl, she was convinced that she'd never come out alive. Finally, in 2008, she was right.

She was ninety-one. I don't know why, specifically, she'd been hospitalised, but I was informed that she'd been admitted, that she was distressed, and that perhaps a visit from me might be welcome.

I drove over from Yorkshire to Pwllheli in my motorhome – a bit cumbersome, but since I was retired and my wife was still working, she had first dibs on the car.

It was a fierce winter's day. Clouds streamed overhead, and I had to wrestle with the steering wheel to avoid being blown either off the road or into oncoming traffic. Approaching Caernarfon, the roof of somebody's shed cartwheeled across in front of me. Shaken, I pulled into Morrisons to get something to eat.

As I rounded one of the car park trolley-bays, a blast of wind rocked the van and a corner of the bay ripped into its side. I vaguely remembered from Swift's 'A' Level lessons the signs and portents in *Macbeth*. They did not bode well in medieval Scotland. Nor, as it turned out, in twenty-first-century Wales.

I sought out the store manager and explained what had happened. She said it was fine to leave the motorhome on the carpark overnight. I locked up, crossed the road to a B&B, booked a room, then went to a nearby pub for a pint. Despite the consolations of alcohol, I couldn't shake off a feeling of gathering doom.

Next morning, I retrieved the van, patched up the hole with gaffer tape (getting stuck in a supermarket carpark has its advantages), continued to Pwllheli and parked outside Penlleiniau, where Mum lived in what had once been the school-house. After I'd unpacked. I set off for Bryn Beryl by bus.

What a palaver.

Mum was in a general ward, very distressed, very relieved to see me. While she seemed in fine form, I felt that there was something not quite right. She was moved, shortly after I arrived, into a single room with views across the fields towards The Rivals. 'This is a lovely room,' I said, trying to cheer her up. 'They must think I'm going to die,' she said glumly.

That night I phoned my brother Chris in London, and he joined me in Penlleiniau the next day. With my late older brother Jeff's first wife Ambo, who lived in Llanystumdwy, we set up a shift system to sit with Mum. The Bryn Beryl staff kindly allowed us to use a small adjoining room with a bed so that our night shift could try to get some sleep, and kept us supplied with hot drinks and sandwiches.

The vigil went on for nearly a week, with Mum getting weaker and suffering bouts of confusion and despair, though without abandoning her sense of humour:

- 'Father, help me!' she cried at one point. 'Anybody's father will do.'

- She looked out of the window and asked me what 'those white things' were. They were sheep.

- She told me off for lying on the floor. I wasn't – I was sitting next to the bed.

She was becoming increasingly distraught. I asked the sister if Mum couldn't be given something to relieve her distress. She said that her current medication precluded it. Her current medication was designed to prolong life, I pointed out. Surely, at ninety-one, and in her anguished state, stress relief was more important? I later found out from Chris that he'd had said the same thing.

We settled into a twenty-four-hour vigil, the three of us taking it in turns to sit and chat with Mum or, when she was asleep, read or do crossword puzzles.

Finally, as I was sitting in the Crossville bus in the Maes in Pwllheli, its engine running, waiting to set off for my night shift, Chris climbed aboard. Ambo had phoned to say that we'd both better get to the hospital as quickly as possible.

Too late. By the time we arrived at Bryn Beryl, Mum was dead.

The hospital staff's were great, and handled everything. They must, of course, be used to it. Chris and I returned to Pwllheli on the bus, went to the Mitre for a pint, then to the basement restaurant across the road in the old *Liverpool Echo* office for a meal. It was sombre, but somehow appropriate.

The following weeks were a blur – seeing to 'the arrangements', the funeral, sorting the house out. It's amazing how much stuff you leave behind you when you die, compared to the total absence of stuff you bring with you when you're born. Apart from the afterbirth and umbilical cord, I suppose. Yet it all seemed so little to show for nearly a hundred years on the planet – a house, some bits of furniture, clothes, some brass candlesticks, a few pictures.

And me and my brother, of course.

Towards the end of her life, Mum used to say of her siblings,

'I was the runt of the litter – nobody expected me to survive my childhood. And now I've outlived them all.' At the time I wasn't sure that her triumphalism was quite appropriate. But why not? Take your victories where you find them. Now, when I'm seventy-seven, I'd settle for ninety-one. Perhaps when I'm ninety I'll change my mind.

Did Mum have 'a good death'? I don't know. I think she would, like most of us, have preferred to die at home. But, compared to passing away in a large impersonal general hospital, Bryn Beryl wasn't a bad compromise. They allowed her to be accompanied to the edge of extinction by members of her family, whom they supplied with food, coffee and a room in which to rest. There was a local Pwllheli feel to it all that wouldn't have been possible in Bangor's C&A. Or was it Ysbyty Gwynedd? I'm not sure when it changed.

That said, as for myself and probably most of the rest of humanity, I'd really rather not die at all.

Bryn Beryl – postscript

When I wrote about my mother's death in Bryn Beryl, it hadn't occured to me that almost everybody in Pwllheli would have similar experiences with elderly parents or other family members. The memories were very affecting:

- My brother chipped in with thoughts about the death of both our parents (and a photograph from before they were married). We both bitterly regret not having asked them more about their lives. And he claims that, after Mum's death, we didn't catch the bus back to Pwllheli, but that Ambo gave us a lift. It always bears remembering that memory can be very slippery indeed.

- A member of the group recalled a telephone conversation he had with his mother shortly before she died. She'd clearly been in the same room as my mother, or a similar one. 'Every time I wake up, there's a bloody big sheep staring at me!'

- The mother of another still worked at Bryn Beryl, at the age of seventy-two. He speculated that this must have been, for her, a daily 'memento mori'.

- Yet another remembered his mother in one of the 'rooms with a view' which she found 'gentle and calming'. Her doctor (Dr Gwenda, my drug supplier) was in the next bed (as a patient, not a staff member), and they were able to cheer each other up. Even holding hands, launching themselves into oblivion. Like Thelma and Louise.

- The daughter of one of the teachers at YRP (Maldwyn) was sad that her father had died in Bryn Beryl in the year that her daughter was born, and that, therefore, they had never known each other. 'She has a little curl in the nape of her neck just like Dad,' she wrote, and just as the memory of Maldwyn's totally bald head was forming in my mind, she added, 'Yes, he did once have hair you know.'

- I'll end this Postscript with a quote that another member of the group contributed: 'We all die. The goal isn't to live for ever, the goal is to create something that will.' This was Chuck Palahniuk (the originator of the quote, not the member of the group), who, Wikipedia tells me, wrote, among other things, *Fight Club*. Wise words.

Beside the sea

I've written often in the past about the pleasures and dangers of living by the sea. Those were pretty 'broad brush' accounts. Since then a lot of less obvious ones have occurred to me.

Pleasures included:

- Sitting on South Beach, sifting through handfuls of sand, looking for tiny shells – often no more than a millimetre long. I would find, say, five or six, then take them home and Sellotape them into the base of a matchbox, as a sort of display case. Now as a hobby, this might seem a bit sad, a bit 'niche', and to my shame I never found out what shells they were, but it satisfied that instinct to collect stuff that seems to be part of being a small boy. Or even a human being.

- Fixing a broken knife for my mother. The bone handle had shattered, leaving just a steel spike that extended from the blade. It was one of a canteen of cutlery of which she was very proud – I think it was a wedding present. I searched the beach for some of the seaweed (kelp? bladderwort?) that Dad had told me about, which he swore had in the past been used for the handles of knives. Having sorted through a slithering pile of brown-green seaweed, I cut a section of the stem to size then slid the spike into its hollow interior. Within a week the stem had dried out and shrunk, sealing it immovably to the spike. This new knife handle looked impressively like bone (though more like the antlers of a stag than the smooth pale bone of the original handle), and I presented the repaired knife to my mother with great pride. She thanked me courteously and laid it in its velvet space in the canteen box. Of course, it looked nothing like the rest of the knives ranked on either side. I never saw the knife again. Easy to be hurt as a child, but as a parent I totally understand.

- The scullery of our house in Llŷn Street leaked every time it rained. Dad and I scoured the beach until we found a huge lump of tar – jettisoned, presumably, from some passing ship. We took it home, Dad melted bits of it in a tin can over the gas stove, and patched the leaking roof. I'd like to say that it never leaked again. But I can't.

- I fetched a sea anemone from a rock-pool on Gimblet Rock and kept it in a glass biscuit-barrel in the garden shed. Out of the water it just looked like a blob of strawberry jam, but when flooded with brine it blossomed like a flower. It lived happily there for many weeks – as the

63

seawater evaporated, I simply had to top it up with fresh water from the tap. In the end, however, it died. I think I'd let the water level drop too much, making the brine too concentrated for the anemone to survive.

Dangers included:

- A gang of us kids trying to keep a tidal gate under the Cob Bridge open by bracing ourselves on the canopy above the gate and pushing with our feet. Six kids, hoping to cancel the gravitational pull of a celestial body a quarter of the size of the earth. The moon won. And Steven Morgan got his foot stuck between the gate and the canopy. We heaved to try to get the gate open a sliver, and when this failed, we hauled hard on Steve himself until he popped out of his wellie like a cork from a champagne bottle. He was free, but his wellie stayed squashed by the gate. I can't remember how he got home – I assume he hopped. How he explained his lost wellie to his parents I've no idea.

- Off the beach at the West End was moored a raft, to which kids would swim, and from which they would dive. I am not the world's best swimmer, but I was too embarrassed to admit this and so swam out with everybody else. When I pulled myself onto the raft, there was no diving off it for me – I was knackered. Finally plucking up the courage for the return journey, I set off back towards the beach. My arms grew heavier and heavier, waves slapped me in the face, I swallowed water. But I flailed away in a sort of demented doggy-paddle until finally I was able to crawl up the beach and flop down on my towel. Why on earth did I insist on swimming out to the raft with everybody else? Why on earth didn't I shout for help when I nearly drowned on the way back? The answer's simple – I was ashamed. Don't let anyone tell you that you can't die of embarrassment.

- I was at a *cymanfa ganu* (singing festival) in Aberdaron,

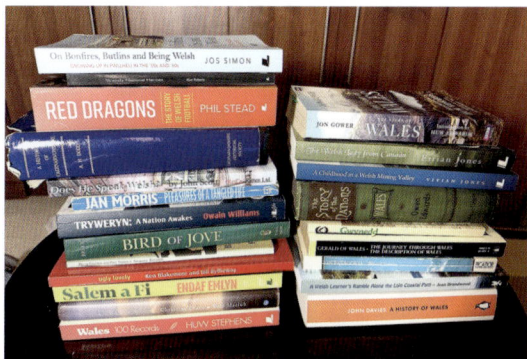

Hiraeth creeps up on you. Accumulation of books about Wales taken at random from my shelves.

PWLLHELI GRAMMAR SCHOOL 1961 – 62

Close-up of YRP staff in panoramic photo (1961–62), illustrating gender imbalance.

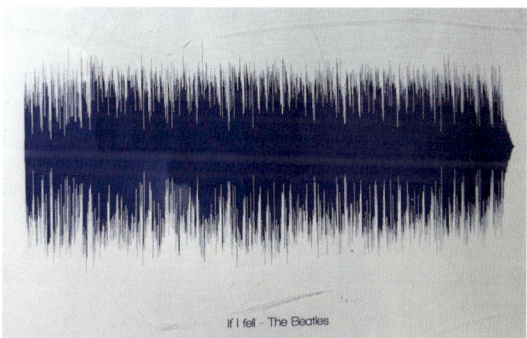

If I fell - The Beatles

Audiograph of 'If I Fell' by the Beatles – a birthday present from my daughter.

Three of my early magazine articles about caravanning in Wales.

Chirk Castle.

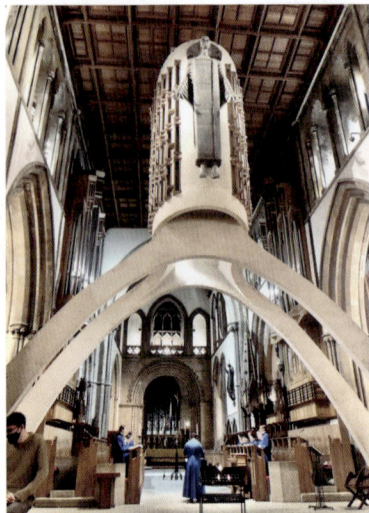

Cardiff: Llandaff Cathedral showing Epstein's *Majestas* and the cathedral girls' choir in rehearsal.

Paris: a few beers on our first rugby trip to Paris – me on the left, next to brother Jeff.

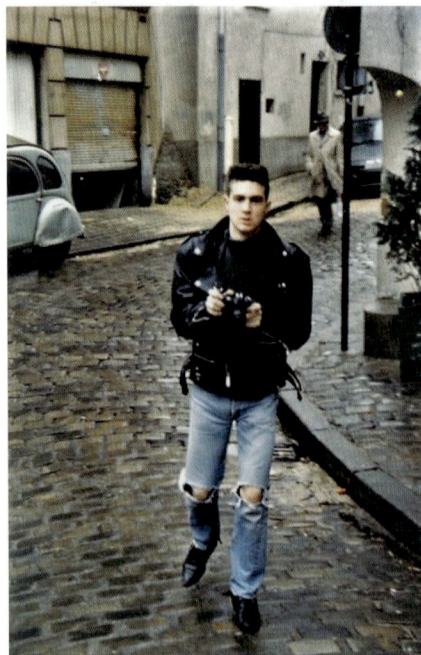

Start of second rugby trip to Paris – son Daniel (aged 16) during breakfast stop in Montmartre.

End of second rugby trip to Paris – son Daniel and the Eiffel Tower (aged just short of 100) on our way home.

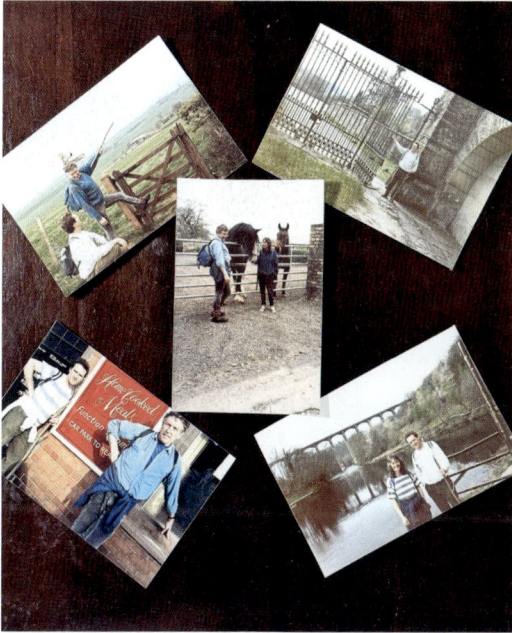

Prints of three-day walk from Newcastle-under-Lyme to Llangollen with Bill and Murph. Top left – Bill showing me the way to Wales. Bottom right – Murph, me and the Pontcysyllte Aqueduct.

Me and my daughter Catherine with south Wales valley (probably Rhondda Fach) in the background.

Brother Chris in Darren Park, Ferndale, on our visit to cousin Christine in Llantwit Major.

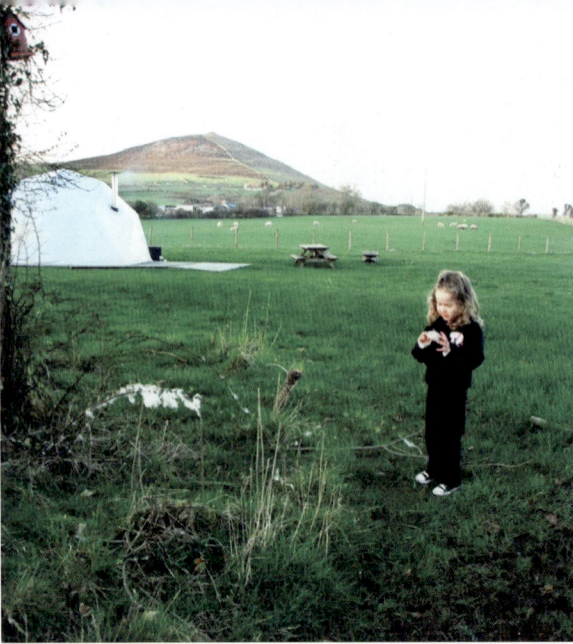

Granddaughter Arianwen on my daughter's fortieth birthday celebration – in a yurt just outside Y Ffôr.

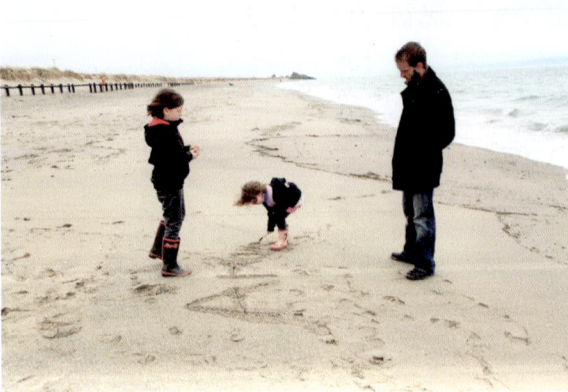

South Beach, Pwllheli – Arianwen writes her name in the sand as dad and sibling look on.

Portmeirion: our golden wedding anniversary with the family – we rented the yellow house next to the tower.

My niece Ceri's wedding just outside Llanystumdwy. Left to right – me, son Daniel, brother Chris.

Swallow Falls: my daughter Catherine.

Swallow Falls: her daughter, my granddaughter, Arianwen, some half-century later.

Chain link bridge just outside Llangollen – left to right, daughter Catherine, Arnaud and son Daniel.

The same three running for the train in Tan-y-Bwlch on the Ffestiniog Railway.

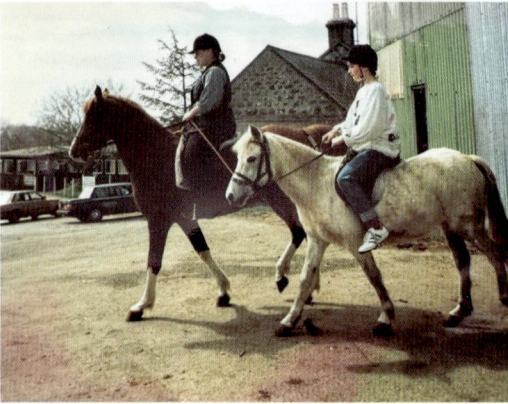

Daughter Catherine and her French exchange student Cecile, heading for the beach in Llanbedrog.

Article in *Yr Enfys*, magazine of 'Wales International'.

A book that makes you feel that bit closer to Wales

by Jos Simon, Author

Towards the end of my thirty-year teaching career I started writing articles for caravan magazines. Early retirement allowed me to expand into less niche outlets which in turn led to guide-book writing - on Croatia, the Greek islands and Crete for Frommers, on Yorkshire and Cyprus for Rough Guides. My favourites were Greece and Cyprus - perhaps because my wife's Greek Cypriot!

Then, half-way up a Mediterranean mountain - short of breath and weary of leg - I decided that travel-writing was best left to the young. It can wear you out, and I was now 70 years old.

In 2019 I started contributing posts to the *Ysgolion Pwllheli and District Schools Facebook group*, about growing up in the town. These sparked off memories in other group members, who chipped in with comments, anecdotes, memories of local characters, even jokes. People reconnected with friends and acquaintances from sixty years ago. Lockdown followed. Posts and comments mushroomed - we all needed something to do.

The posts alone built up a picture of life in Pwllheli and Llŷn in the mid-twentieth century. But the depth and scope of that picture was hugely enhanced by the comments they provoked. So I added 'Postscripts'. Some members suggested that I should collect the posts and comments into a book, then that Welsh publishers *Y Lolfa* might be interested. I did, and they were!

The book is made up of stories. For example:

- of the pitched battles across the town in the run-up to bonfire night.
- of a magical trip with my father to Aberdaron to pick up a Christmas turkey, where the family talked in the farmhouse kitchen about their delight that the TV news was now in Welsh, their disappointment that the weather forecast was still in English.
- of a farm girl so terrorised by the turkeys as she got home from school that her mother had to send the dogs out to protect her. She got her own back, of course, on Christmas day. Revenge, in this case at least, was a dish best served hot.
- of a young girl waiting to be baptised by total immersion in the pool beneath the 'sêt fawr', wearing a borrowed dress and with 'a powdery swirl leaking out of my newly whitened plimsolls'. The chapel today? A furniture and bric-a-brac showroom.
- of making taffars, of scouring the local tip for parts to make go-carts, of diving off Gimblet Rock, of underage drinking, of seeing The Beatles at the Odeon, Llandudno.

Finally, a word about the Welsh diaspora. When trying to estimate the likely turnout at a proposed book-signing in Pwllheli, I checked where members of the group actually live. In Pwllheli, certainly, but also all over the UK and even the world - China, California, Copenhagen, Tasmania, Greece, Germany, France, Italy!

I loved the idea that our book might stir the embers of 'hiraeth', might help us all, wherever we live, feel that bit closer to Wales. It reminded me of an early internet strapline: 'Geography is history'!

And I'd love to write a sequel, but that rather depends, not only on how well this book sells, but how many more memories of growing up on Llŷn that the YPDS group can shake loose!

On Bonfires, Butlins and Being Welsh by Jos Simon (£9.99, *Y Lolfa*) is available now.

The Welsh Language and Heritage Centre, Nant Gwrtheyrn.

Llŷn Inland.

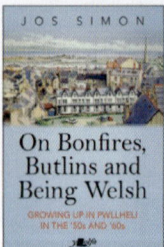

JOS SIMON

On Bonfires, Butlins and Being Welsh

GROWING UP IN PWLLHELI IN THE '50s AND '60s

Jos's children on South Beach, Pwllheli.

Gimblet Rock, Pwllheli.

St Peter's Church, Pwllheli.

Bron-y-Wendon, Llanddulas: Our Little Welsh Home in the West.

View from the static – rainbow over the Gwynt-y-Môr wind farm. North Wales railway line in the foreground.

Another view from the static – evening clouds over the Little Orme.

Granddaughter Arianwen flipping stones in the Dulas river, just below Bron-y-Wendon campsite.

Arianwen researching for her first trip to Llandudno.

Porth Eirias: environmental cormorant made of odd bits of bikes, tyres, flippers and other odds and ends.

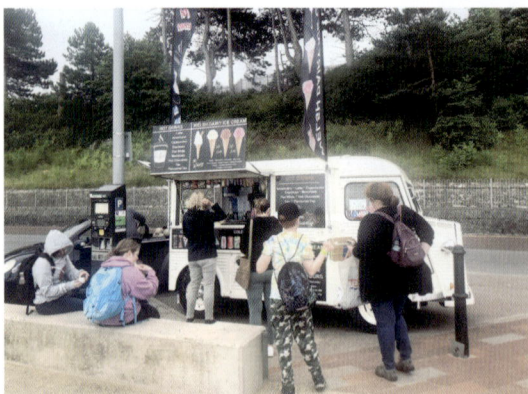

Ice-cream van on the prom at Old Colwyn.

Arianwen and her grandmother at the Welsh Mountain Zoo in Bae Colwyn. Arianwen on the left.

Llandudno: young man shows his grandmother how hopscotch is played, with other members of the family and a seagull looking on.

Llandudno is for the kids.

Llandudno's Victorian Extravaganza.

But Llandudno is also for us oldies – it must be the bench capital of the UK, for which I'm really, really grateful.

Asked whether she'd like to have a go on this ride, Arianwen said, 'I'd rather die.'

Llandudno's famous Kashmiri goats, hanging about outside Asda.

Llandudno's 'Venue Cymru'
– granddaughter Arianwen attending a show with a friend. A birthday treat.

The Great Orme Prehistoric Copper Mines – an unexpected hit.

The quay at Conwy, with the castle in the background.

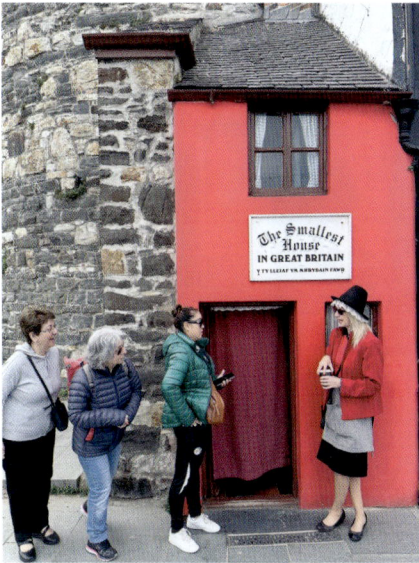

Conwy's smallest house in Britain. Wife and sister-in-law behind a visitor in the queue.

Conwy: the steps up to the Jester's Tower, with its excellent café and beautiful views of the estuary.

Conwy: the Knight's Shop. Warning – if you allow children in, it's not easy to get them to leave.

Conwy's beautiful Marine Walk.

Gimblet Rock, Pwllheli: the family with guest Emma.

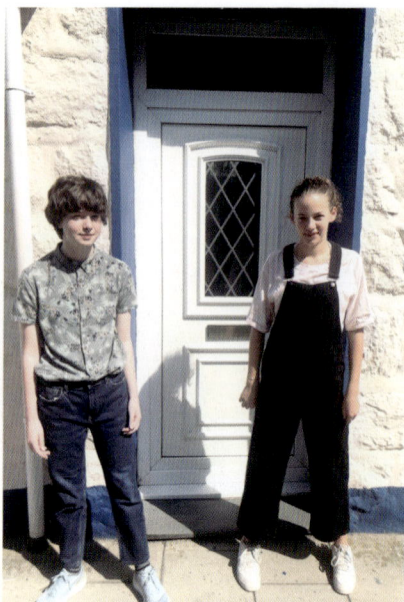

Pwllheli: Arianwen with Emma outside the erstwhile Bank Place Hotel, where Emma's grandfather Tony Pierce was brought up.

Tony Pierce's granddaughter Emma with my grandchildren Arianwen and Lazaros outside what used to be Pwllheli's Liberal Club.

The grandchildren outside Pwllheli Town Hall.

Emma with what was Penlleiniau School (now flats) in the background, where my father was the headteacher for forty years, and where I and my brothers attended school.

My stolen dictionary, Emma (the thief's emissary) and myself, trying to express our disappointment at this historical felony.

Emma dealing with the fact that the handle of the knife with which she was cutting my son Daniel's fiftieth birthday cake came off! My son-in-law Matt failing to hide his amusement.

Nanhoron Arms Hotel, Nefyn: the family enjoying Dan's fiftieth birthday meal.

The walk along the cliffs after the meal.

Towards the end of Emma's stay in Llanddulas – a morning walk with Arianwen next to the Dulas river.

Extract from a Literary Map of Wales. The full map contains a staggering amount of information on one sheet of paper!

Some of my travel books by Jan Morris.

Boduan eisteddfod – general view.

Boduan eisteddfod – the Y Lolfa tent.

My shares in Y Tŵr.

and had some spare time to wander around the village. In the churchyard that slopes down to the beach, I saw the graves of sailors lost at sea, many little older than I was. The lesson was clear – don't mess with the sea.

That said, I would dearly love to live by the sea. But where did life's tides, the currents of education and career, the unpredictable eddies of children and grandchildren, deposit me? A place noticeable for a total absence of beaches, and as far from the sea as you can get! Stoke-on-Trent!

Beside the sea – postscript

I suppose that, since we all lived on a narrow peninsula jutting out into the Irish Sea, with Cardigan Bay to the south, Liverpool Bay to the north, it was inevitable that the sea played a large part in our growing up. Comments included:

- A description of idyllic summer days spent on the traeth at Trefor, making friends with visitors, enjoying frequent revisits during adulthood and the pain of the interruption of these visits by lockdown.

- The celebration of so many great beaches within ten miles, and, from one group member, a sad admission – 'I always wanted to live by the sea, and ended up in Doncaster.' As, between two periods of living in Stoke, did I!

- Others were much luckier – one who was brought up on the harbourside in Pwllheli, went to college on the shores of Lake Windermere and now lives on the sound between Denmark and Sweden. 'Not consciously chosen – it just seemed to happen.' Kissed by the gods!

- On a more personal note, my brother commented that my father's attempts to patch the scullery roof with tar off the beach having obviously failed, his next attempt involved sheathing the whole roof in corrugated plastic. Which also failed.

65

- And finally, a comment that has haunted me since I read it. A member of the group explained that sea anemones feed on plankton. By topping up the buiscuit-barrel from the tap I was replenishing the water, but not the food. The sea anemone starved to death. It died of ignorance. Mine. Although I berated myself, he was very kind. Refering both to the death of my pet sea anemone and my near-drowning off the beach at West End, he said, 'We only *live* by the sea. It does not make us marine biologists or born swimmers. Don't be too harsh on yourself.' I could have sobbed with gratitude. I hope the sea anemone is equally forgiving.

A Local Town for Local People

Looking back on growing up in Pwllheli in the 1950s and '60s, I'm impressed with how *local* our lives were. Even the chainstores (Woolworths, W H Smiths, Stead & Simpson) *felt* local. And a lot of things really were:

- When the pedal shaft on my bike snapped, Dad took me and the bike to a place just across Upper Ala Road from the police station. It was some sort of engineering works – farm machinery, that sort of thing. They welded it back on – good as new. Ever since I've though of welding as a sort of magic.

- And when my school satchel started to fall apart, the saddler who lived further up Llŷn Street stitched it back together for me. It lasted till I left school.

- When I was bunged up with cold, Dad took me to the gasworks, where I was suspended over the tar pit to clear my sinuses. I was held (not firmly enough, it seemed to me) a few feet above foul bubbling black tar, and instructed to breath deeply. It did, I have to admit, ease my breathing. If I'd been constipated, it would have eased that as well.

- When our family's shoes became the worse for wear, I was sent off to Ensors, just off the Maes, for them to be resoled or reheeled. I didn't mind – I loved the smell of leather.

- The local undertaker was also a joiner on the Maes (Jenkins? His wife was active in local am dram?). He not only conducted the funerals, he also built the coffins. I think it's called vertical integration. He handled Dad's funeral, and, shortly afterwards, that of the vicar who'd officiated. His own funeral, I seem to remember, wasn't far behind. I loved that – locals easing their own into the great beyond, in a sort of infinite progression.

- You could buy fish off Jack Ben's cart. You knew that the little corpses were fresh – they'd have been quick with life, foraging in Cardigan Bay that very morning.

- And local businesses seemed to be run by local people. Entrepreneurs, finding and filling the gaps in the market. Take my friend Ginge's dad, Mr Martin. Though not local, he married a Pwllheli girl, settled in the town, and opened a chip shop, a sweet shop and a bike shop. He added a huge amount to the life of the town, not only through his enterprises, but through his children. It was the same for the Mr Pierce and the Bank Place Hotel, for Thornton's, for Polecoffs, for many others.

- On a visit long after I'd left Pwllheli, I was having a coffee above Spar in the Maes. At another table was a group of blokes – retired businessmen, managers, professionals (my old dentist Mr Cowell was one of them) – and they all obviously knew each other well. They were talking about golfing trips, jaunts to London, upcoming events in the town, with much banter and laughter. Freemasons? Round table? I don't know. But it all seemed so enviably inclusive. And so enviably local.

The big conglomerates are moving in. Small local businesses wither away in their shade. Something should be done!

This, of course, is our job – us oldies. To moan about the way things are going. Now, let me tell you what I think about tattoos, false eyelashes and electric scooters.

A Local Town for Local People – postscript

Writing about miscellaneous memories is a bit like fishing, casting your line into deep waters – you never know what further memories you're going to pull out of the past – your own or somebody else's. This time:

- The magicians who fixed my bike were identified as a company called Pierce-Jones.

- Prompted by that story, a member of the group remembered coming off his racer one weekend as he rode too fast down the steep incline from Rhiw to Porth Neigwl (Hell's Mouth, as it is more colourfully called in English). Having dragged the twisted wreckage back up the hill to a local garage, to be picked up later, he asked the proprietor, 'What time's the next bus?' Looking at his watch he said, deadpan, 'Wednesday.'

- This story in turn led to a flood of memories of the bus companies, big and small, that served Llŷn's towns, villages and hamlets – God bless them, God damn them, and how we miss them now that most of them are gone.

- It was observed that, even as late as the 1950s, and even in a rural area like ours, the saddler who lived up our street fixed more satchels than saddles, horses having become a luxury rather than the necessity that once they were. His single review (apart from mine) as a bag repairer, though, was glowing. A backpack to which he attached new straps survived a punishing tour of Norway unscathed and, I think, survives to this day.

- Mention of the undertaker/joiner led to a flurry of

memories. His full surname was Jenkin-Evans. and Betty Jenkin-Evans his wife was indeed a fervent member of the local am dram group, The Kew Minstrels – she was a vivid character, an extrovert thesp. The brother of one of our members was, as a young man, appreticed to Mr Jenkin-Evans, both as joiner and undertaker, and took over when he died. He hated it when, raring to go out on a Saturday night, he might have to build a coffin instead. Tragically, he himself died in a motor-cycle accident at the age of twenty-four. Another member of the group, before leaving Pwllheli for music college, played trumpet in the pit orchestra to whose music the Kew Minstrels performed. 'Under the baton,' she said, 'of Eric Williams.' No jokes please. If I remember rightly, Eric was YRP's music teacher.

- My brief but terrifying visit to the gasworks tar-pit provoked merchant navy memories of the traditional tarring-and-feathering of young ratings on their first crossing of the equator. I sometimes forget that Pwllheli is a nautical town.

Penrhos Camp

I've recently seen press reports of the death of Penrhos Camp. Until I read them, I didn't realise how little I knew about the camp or how much a part of my growing up in Pwllheli it, and the Polish community it housed, had been. Who knew?

No doubt whatever's happening must be necessary – the world moves on. But I can't help thinking that, as Penrhos Camp fades back into history, Pwllheli will be the poorer for its departure.

Ashamed at my ignorance about the camp and its origins, I did some research:

- Penrhos Camp started life in the 1930s when the Air Ministry bought a farm (Penyberth) upon which to develop an airfield to be devoted in general to weapons training, and in particular to the establishment of a bombing school.

- This development led to an iconic episode of Welsh history. *Tân yn Llŷn* involved the burning of one of the buildings of the military installation by Saunders Lewis, Lewis Valentine and D J Williams in 1936. It was a protest against its location (in the Welsh-language heartland), its purpose (to develop what many considered to be a barbarous method of warfare) and the fact that two other proposed sites (in Northumberland and Dorset) had been abandoned because of violent local protest. The three men, who immediately went to Pwllheli police station to give themselves up, were eventually sentenced to nine months in prison. Their sacrifice had no effect on the authorities (one law for England, another law for Wales?) but they became widely celebrated as heroes in their homeland.

- When the war ended, Penrhos Camp was used as a temporary demobilisation base for thousands of Polish soldiers and airmen. When it became clear that many Poles couldn't, or wouldn't, return to Poland, the camp became a permanent home to many Polish servicemen and to their refugee compatriots displaced by the war.

So much for how Pwllheli happened to have a bombing school, then Polish enclave, a couple of miles west of the town. But how did it affect us kids as we grew up in the 1950s and '60s?

- The most obvious relic of the bombing school was the 'target' – a huge pyramid that sat out in the bay. Wooden-clad when I was a child, it was later stripped of its timber to reveal a gigantic steel tripod (big enough for large pleasure-boats to sail comfortably underneath). I'd always imagined airmen, scarves streaming behind them, leaning out of Lancaster bombers, pitching sacks of dye at it, splashing it with colour when they hit it or staining the sea around it when they missed. In old age I realise that it was probably a bit more technical than that. After I left Pwllheli the tripod disappeared. I hope nobody thought I'd nicked it.

- We were all, as kids, aware of a Polish dimension to our town. For example, we'd see old Polish men sitting in or outside cafés reading Polish newspapers. I remember a very elderly man sitting at one of the tables outside Brexo, earnestly working through his newspaper with the aid of a huge magnifying glass.

- Polish kids at school had names which seemed even more full of consonants than Welsh ones were.

- The cemetery in Denio had a whole section of Polish headstones, again with tongue-twisting names. I've since thought how sad it must be to die so far from home.

- The Tu Hwnt i'r Afon pub in Rhyd-y-clafdy, close to the camp's rear entry, had all its notices in Welsh, English – and Polish. Towards the end of his life, I used to go there with dad. He liked a drink (the odd half) and loved to play the fruit machine. But, being head of a church school, he had to get well clear of Pwllheli to indulge. Though he *had* been known to sneak into the Castle on the High Street through the back door (which, I'm told, was known as the 'Deacon's Entrance').

- When the Polish Pope John Paul II (the less easily remembered Karol Jósef Wojtyla) visited the UK, community leaders from Penrhos were helicoptered out to meet him, representing what was, I think, the largest Polish community in the UK.

I did visit Penrhos Camp at some point – I remember a well-ordered 1950s-type housing estate – but I can't remember why. It might have been when I was learning to drive. I heard that, because the roads on the camp hadn't been 'adopted', a lot of driving instructors took their more nervous novices there for their first drive. More realistic driving conditions than Black Rock Sands, but less harrowing than the busy streets of Pwllheli. I don't know what the Polish community thought of this.

Penrhos Camp – postscript

Comments arising from the post painted a very positive picture of relations between the Polish community and the surrounding area:

- The use of the camp for driving lessons was clearly fairly common. One comment I found particularly interesting – my younger brother Chris explains that our older brother Jeff (who was sixteen years his senior) gave him driving lessons on the roads of Penrhos Camp, presumably when he was too young to get a licence to drive on ordinary roads.
- Alcohol too was a common thread:
  o One group member's mother, who worked in a wine shop on Pwllheli High Street, said that they had to stock a particularly fierce type of vodka specifically for Polish men.
  o This prompted another to remember being asked by his Polish neighbour, while she was on holiday, to 'water' her plants with neat vodka. She also, perhaps as payment for this good deed, encouraged him to try it himself, mixed with apple juice. 'It tasted deliciously like apple strudel,' he reports, 'but acted like a rocket.'
  o And further to the alcohol theme, the landlord of the Castle in Pwllheli's High Street was, at one time, Polish as his name attests: Leo Wisniewski.
- There were strong musical connections between the camp and the local area:

o One member of our Facebook group, while studying for 'A' Level music at Ysgol Ramadeg Pwllheli was, with others, taken by much-loved music teacher Eric Williams to the camp to meet a Chopin expert, who would talk to them about the great composer, play his music for them, and feed them Lebkuchen biscuits.

o Another filled in some detail – the Chopin expert's name was Jan, and he worked as a caretaker in Llanbedrog Village Hall.

o Further memories followed – of local school choirs and orchestras performing for the people of the camp, of how much this was appreciated, and of how tearful many of the elderly Poles became at such recitals (for example at a rendering of 'Edelweiss' by one of the girls).

• Another memory was of its time. In the early 1960s a member of the group used to be sent on his bike to buy eggs at the Co-op egg-packing station which had been established at the camp. The standardised eggs were stamped with a red lion (remember those?), but others that failed the standardisation test – misshapen, say, or with double yolks – were sold off cheaply. And none the worse for that, apparently.

• The same member and his friends found the abandoned RAF part of the site an ideal place to play war games among the surviving huts, rolls of barbed wire and other relics of the old bombing school. He remembered their excitement at finding one hut with a faded name on the door, starting with 'A' and ending with 'ion Hut'. Imagining their disappointment when it turned out to be, not the 'Ammunition Hut', full of bullets, shells and grenades that they'd hoped for, but the 'Ablution Hut', full of cracked porcelain and ruptured pipes. Good job, I'd have thought, or they might not have been around to tell the tale!

- A member of the group noted that recently the Catholic Church on Penrhos Camp has lost its priest, so that its Polish worshippers had to be bussed to St Joseph's in Pwllheli's South Beach every Sunday. The incumbent (Nigerian) priest now greets the congregation in Welsh, Polish and English, in that order!

- Her husband remembered, as a child, that his dad, together with a Polish airman friend, sent the kids off to Saturday matinée at the Palladium to get them out of the way, then slaughtered a pig in the bath. Not the usual stuff of nostalgia, perhaps, but the memory of bacon, sausages and heavenly pork for weeks afterwards lived in the memory until – well – today.

- Finally, some more sombre memories:
  o Poles on the camp were apparently keen jumble-sale attenders, not on the lookout for bargains for themselves, but in order to buy clothes cheaply to send to relatives in Poland.
  o Many of the ex-servicemen on the site had been officers in the Polish forces, and claimed to be in danger of execution if they returned to their Russian-dominated homeland. And, given what we now know about the Katyn Massacre of over 20,000 Polish officers, policemen and members of the intelligentsia by the Soviet Union in 1940, who can blame them?
  o As mentioned in the post, when they died, Poles from Penrhos Camp were buried at Denio cemetery, on a hill above Pwllheli. Several members of the group remembered Polish funerals. For the earlier ones, mourners were transported to the cemetery by coach; later on, by minibus, and eventually, by car.

History tells us that, during the Second World War, the Poles were welcomed as heroes fighting shoulder-to-shoulder with the British against Nazi tyranny. After the war, as the large number of Polish servicemen in the UK were joined by their families and dependents, as post-war austerity caused by the huge cost of the war set in, there was a marked shift in attitude, with some seeing the Poles as foreign interlopers, as a drain on the country's limited resources.

It's interesting that this negative view isn't reflected in the memories of those of us who grew up in Pwllheli after the war. We seem to view the Polish community positively, sympathising with its residents being so far from home, applauding it for its contribution to the war and to our childhood. Indeed, I detect a sadness that this contribution is coming to an end.

CHAPTER 3

People we knew, relationships we had

IN SOME WAYS, memories of the things we did and the places we knew when we were growing up are the easiest to handle. Memories of people and relationships can be more difficult.

Some time ago in a post I mentioned a kid I quite liked in primary school, and the cute costume his mother had dressed him in for Pwllheli carnival. Hadn't seen him since then. Now, seventy years later, his daughter chipped in with, 'The bastard left us when we were toddlers and Mum was pregnant with my younger brother.'

So you've got to be careful.

Fathers and sons

When you get old, you look back over your relationship with your parents, your relationship with your own kids, your own kids' relationship with *their* kids. Have you avoided mistakes you felt your parents made, only to make your own? Are your kids avoiding the mistakes *you* made, only to make their own mistakes in their turn? It really makes you think.

My father could be very overbearing, and as I grew up I had many reasons to curse his insistence on having his own way:

- My friends had racing bikes – light frames, drop handlebars, tiny saddles, derailer gears, narrow wheels with slim tyres, and lights powered by hub dynamos. For passing the eleven plus, I got a second-hand bike from Martin's – heavy steel frame, traditional handlebars, great wedge of a saddle, Sturmey-Archer gears, fat wide rims with fat wide tyres, and lights powered by a bottle-like gismo that you had to click onto the rear tyre, and which made it even harder to peddle, especially up hills. And Pwllheli might not be in Eryri, but there were plenty of hills around.

- My friends had sexy wristwatches, the thinner the better. They looked so cool. But Dad insisted that, because their working parts were severely miniaturised, they were unreliable. I ended up with a pocket watch! Fine if you were a Victorian factory owner or a toff at a London club, with a gold hunter and an impressive watch chain and fob. But I was a schoolboy in 1960s Pwllheli. *My* watch was a great lump of chrome, an Ingersoll whose dial was a footballer kicking a ball, which spun on its axis and was the second hand. Since I had no waistcoat in whose pocket I could keep the watch, it lived in my trouser pocket, secured by a leather strap attached to my belt.

- My older brother had a guitar, on which he was being taught chords by his friend John Prys. I really wanted to learn myself – not only because Jeff was my admired elder brother, but because being able to play an instrument was the key to popularity with friends, success with the opposite sex, and eventual prosperity, super-stardom, and entry into the rock-and-roll hall of fame. Dad should have appreciated this – didn't he meet Mum when she was dancing at the Rink in Ferndale to a band in which Dad was the pianist? But no. I needed to learn chords on a simpler instrument, he said. So I got a blue and white ukulele with a picture on the front of a Mexican sitting under a tree. Eric Clapton may have started on such an instrument. But I doubt it.

77

These were tough things to impose on an adolescent. Yet I loved my bike, I enjoyed the eccentricity of my pocket watch and, although my ukulele did little for my image, I did learn chords which were easily adapted, not long afterwards, to the guitar. As far as I know, nobody took the piss about my bike, my pocket watch, my ukulele. Perhaps they did behind my back, I don't know. Even if they did, perhaps it led me to embrace the eccentric – when everybody else bought 'Kiss me quick' cowboy hats in Rhyl (or was it Llandudno?), I bought a pith helmet.

So thanks to Dad for giving me something to kick against, though that's not how it felt at the time. And apologies to my children for never offering advice, about anything, and so giving them nothing at all to kick against.

Let's hear it for grandparents, parents, children. We all do our best!

Fathers and sons – postscript

Who knew that resentment of parents ran so deep and lasted so long! Comments included:

- My younger brother complaining, not only that the bike he got for Christmas – a Moulton Mini with small wheels – wasn't 'cool' enough, but that having our father holding the saddle as he rode it down Llŷn Street was undignified. He'd rather have fallen off!

- Although another member of the group also had a first bike that was both sturdy and second-hand (neither desirable qualities), her main complaint was that her father wouldn't let her have a 'space hopper'. Though, to her credit, on reflection she felt that 'Dad was right on that one.' Other memories of space hoppers abounded – somebody even posted pictures.

- Further comment involved an odd inversion of the usual complaint – a father who bought his son a state-of-the-art racing bike. Friends with 'clunkers' were free to throw them carelessly down, even ride them into the sea, while he would enviously look on while cursing the need to look after his 'thoroughbred' machine. Sometimes dads just can't win!

- Finally, a member of the group had a grandfather who was 'an engineering god' whose advice led to a magnificent Raleigh Tour de France racer and a Seiko watch. The first led to 'a thin layer of my DNA' coating the roads around Pwllheli, while the watch's 'glow-in-the-dark' dial 'probably had the half-life of yellow cake uranium'. Sometimes granddads just can't win either!

Claims to fame

Whenever one of those conversations start up – you know the ones, the 'claims to fame' conversations – I find myself at a disadvantage. Indeed, for a long time the only claim to fame I could muster was that I had family members or friends with more impressive claims to fame than mine.

For instance:

- Older brother Jeff gave Ringo Starr a cigarette. Steady – I know this is setting the bar rather high. Jeff was sweeping the road in Butlins outside one of the music bars – the Rock and Calypso, I think – when Ringo, then drummer for Rory Storm and the Hurricanes, came out and asked him for a ciggie. Jeff complied. What with Ringo being swept (pun intended), shortly afterwards, to stardom with the Beatles, I think that the cigarette must have slipped his mind – he forgot to return the favour. Worked out as a proportion of total wealth, I reckon Ringo owes my brother several million pounds.
- Jeff had a further claim to fame – he played football with Richard Burton. Though that might be stretching it a bit. Jeff and some other lads were kicking a ball around in a street in Ferndale, the Rhondda pit village where my

grandparents lived, when Burton came out of a house – presumably that of his first wife Sybil, who was a Ferndale girl. The ball ran to Burton, who punted it back to the boys. Wow!

- Younger brother Chris met Rupert Davies in the antique shop across the road to our house. Chris spent a lot of time in the shop, run by childless Mr and Mrs Parker, who sort of adopted him. Many younger Facebook members will know nothing about Rupert Davies, but he was a big star in the 1960s, mainly for his role as Maigret in a hugely popular hit television series. If it's still available somewhere in the ether, check it out – I seem to remember it was very good. Although born in Liverpool, Rupert Davies was of Welsh stock, and eventually bought a holiday home just outside Nefyn. A heavy pipe-smoker, he died in 1976, and at his request, was buried in Pistyll churchyard. This was, of course, after, not before, Chris met him.

- My mother and Auntie Eva spent an evening in Rhondda Golf Club, not far from Ferndale, chatting chummily with Stanley (later Sir Stanley) Baker, another big star who later generations may not remember. His most famous film was *Zulu* in which he played the lead. Mum couldn't get over that she and her sister were swapping cigarettes with him, and calling him 'Stan'. Baker was from Ferndale, and was at one time a big mate and drinking companion of Richard Burton. They fell out over Burton's treatment of Sybil (also, as I said, from Ferndale) when he went off with that hussy Elizabeth Taylor. A heavy smoker, Stanley Baker died of lung cancer (also in 1976 – a bad year for Welsh thespian smokers). Although he met his end in Spain, at his request his ashes were scattered on the mountain above his birthplace.

- Finally, moving on to members of my family-by-marriage, I come to my wife, whose main claim to fame trumps all the others. While at a small convent school in the south of England, she used to be invited by one of her co-pupils to the rather posh house in Kent of her aunt (that's the co-pupil's aunt, not my wife's), Welsh singer Dorothy Squires. And not even that is her principal claim to fame. Dorothy Squires was married to Roger Moore, twelve years her junior. They used to sit around the swimming pool with 'Uncle Roger', who, my wife tells me, was 'uniquely beautiful'. She hadn't at that time, of course, met me.

- Her other, less impressive claim to fame was that she met Margaret Thatcher when the then Education Secretary opened the Suffolk primary school at which my wife taught. The staff all wore red, to make a less-than-subtle political point. Not only did Maggie not notice (or pretended not to notice) the prevalence of red, she also mistook my wife (who was at the time in her mid-twenties but is well under five foot tall) for one of the children.

- One final wife-related claim to fame. I knew that my wife's sister worked for the *Daily Express* as a copy-taker. In those days, before all the electronic bells and whistles of the modern age, sports reporters would phone in their copy, often against the deafening roar of the crowd, and she would type it up (phenomenally quickly) and pass it on to the sub-editors. She one day dropped into a conversation we were having that she frequently took copy from Barry John, who reported rugby matches for the paper. If she'd said that she had a hotline to God, I couldn't have been more flabberghasted. 'What's he like?' I asked. 'Lovely,' she said, 'A real gentleman.'

- Which brings me to my friends, and a claim-to-fame which some might feel eclipses even my wife's, though that depends on whether you're a James Bond fan or a Beatles fan. As was inevitable, it was my cool mate Tony

81

Pierce who challenged my wife's Uncle Roger story. Tony went out with Linda Ness, a tall Scandinavian blonde, and a close friend of John Lennon's. She had letters written to her by Lennon, which included some of his sketches (the one I remember was of a man nailed to a cross, who's saying 'Oh Christ!' Or was it, 'What a way to spend Easter!'). It is even claimed (though she denies it) that Lennon's song 'Norwegian Wood' was a reference to her background. As if this wasn't enough, Linda was related to Eliot Ness, the leader of the Chicago 'Untouchables', who helped to bring down Al Capone. I really hope she was impressed with the calibre of Tony's friends – she it was who, in Swansea, cooked the spaghetti Bolognese that I was eating when I sneezed and expelled it explosively through my nose.

Ringo Starr! Richard Burton! Rupert Davies! Stanley Baker! Roger Moore! Barry John! John Lennon! Eliot Ness! Al Capone! Among all these claim to fame heavy-hitters, I desperately hunted through my own memories of the past to try to top them. And this was what I came up with:

One summer in the 1970s, when I lived in Ipswich and was a keen supporter of the town's football team, I phoned Portman Road to find out when the season started. Remember, this was in the days before the internet, so you couldn't just look it up. *And* when Ipswich Town were a force to be reckoned with. The phone rang, and, in his unmistakable Geordie accent, Bobby Robson answered. He'd actually picked up the phone himself! What a guy! In awed tones I put my question. He answered, 'Saturday after next,' and hung up!

Best I could do.

Claims to fame – postscript
This post led to a veritable tsunami of claims to fame.

Let's start with things my brother Chris told me:

- When working at a benefit office in a fashionable part

of London, Chris met loads of celebrities signing on to cover their stamps. He refused to reveal which ones – the Official Secrets Act, you know – and despite my most severe big brother pressure, he has refused to name them. Very disappointing.

- Chris handed Steven Gately (of Boyzone, he tells me) a tissue. I didn't ask, and dread to think why, or for what.

- Chris appeared on stage with Elton John and Heather Small (him I've heard of, her I haven't). Where, when or why, again I've no idea. You have to work with what you've got.

That's it, I thought. Eclipsed by my kid brother.

But there was so many more to come:

- A member of the group ran a tombola stall with Ioan Gruffudd and Matthew Rhys at Ysgol Gymraeg, Llundain. I responded by asking her, if they got in touch, to mention my book. She replied, 'I will, but they won't.'

- Another member, a resident of Ruthin, had nothing but praise for Rhys Ifans who, she said, you were likely to come across in the local Tesco. He was brought up in the area, has never forgotten his roots, and was a governor of a local special school. Really impressed with this claim to fame, but I can't get past his (or rather, Spike's) underpants in *Notting Hill*.

- I, a Welshman, still struggle to differentiate between Ioan Gruffudd, Matthew Rhys and Rhys Ifans. How the English manage I hate to think.

Other claims to fame included Edwina Curry (OK) and Gino di Campo (who?).

My final 'claim to fame' postscript is a list of the great and the good, and all from one member of the group:

- Spike Milligan, Omar Sharif, Jimmy Carter, Daniel Craig, James Taylor, Andy Warhol, R S Thomas, Richard Branson, Victor Spinetti, Julian Bream, Honor

Blackman, Leslie Philips, Prince Charles, Jan Morris, Bryn Terfel and Duffy. And that's just the ones I'd heard of.

I admit, I challenged this list with a degree of scepticism. After all, we Welsh have a reputation for, shall we say, being economical with the truth.

But the response was persuasive:

'Met, wined and dined with, baby-sat, was in conversaion with, attended a significant occasion with, served, lent a book to, and answered a question by A J P Taylor at Bangor University on a trip with Brasso.'

Another Brasso fan! Fair enough.

A local celebrity: Endaf Emlyn

In searching for claims to fame we naturally ransacked our minds for stars of TV, stage, screen or popular music. But there was no need to look that far afield. There was one such person who walked among us, who was hiding in plain sight.

Many people of my age who attended Ysgol Ramedeg Pwllheli will remember Endaf Emlyn. He later became a well-known broadcaster, folk singer and cinematographer (his 1993 film *Gadael Lenin* won the audience vote for the most popular British film at the London Film Festival). My own memories of him are, however, sketchy, partly because he was a year ahead of me in school, and partly because I had no idea how famous he would become. If I'd known, I'd have paid more attention.

My main impression of Endaf was that he was very intelligent, very good looking and very blond. But also eccentric.

My specific memories boil down to three incidents, all in the sixth form, all trivial. But they were, I think, indicative, of what he was like:

- During a time when Boss had decided to have a crackdown on standards – school uniform, hair length and so on – Endaf came to school with a bottle-green school cap perched ridiculously on top of his thatch of blond hair. This was as subtle a V-sign as I've ever encountered. Nobody wore a school cap to school, except perhaps first years who were wet behind the ears and had over-enthusiastic and ultra-conformist parents. The cap was very small – I'm sure they weren't sold in any but the smallest size because, and I have to emphasize this, *nobody above the first year would be seen dead wearing a school cap.* So there stood Endaf, a tall sixth former, with this tiny bottle-green cap sitting on top of his golden haystack of hair. And what could the head do about it? It was a clearly stated part of school uniform, and the fact that it was worn satirically couldn't be proved. So, deciding that discretion was the better part of valour, he ignored Endaf's challenging grin and the titters of us onlookers, turned around with a swirl of his cape and stalked off.

- Sixth formers had 'prep' in the school hall/library. Endaf and I were sitting opposite each other at the same table. Without warning, he flicked his fountain pen, sending a line of inkblots diagonally across my face. Though he was older than me (yes, I know. But 'I' seems far too pedantic), this required a response. I slowly took a bottle of blue Quink out of my satchel, filled my fountain pen with ink, then laid it on the table, like a loaded gun. As he kept a wary eye on the pen, I poured the rest of the bottle over his head. This was all done in total silence (it was the library, after all). We separately went to the toilet and cleaned ourselves up. And never mentioned what had happened, even after school. At the time I thought it was odd. Now the word that springs to mind is 'surreal'.

- I was in the same 'A' Level History group as Endaf. Since he was a year ahead of me, this requires some explanation:
  - o Because YRP was a small school (about 450 pupils) with a proportionately small sixth form, subjects

were, where possible, doubled up. So, in 'A' Level History, first and second years were taught together.

o Furthermore, the school couldn't afford enough textbooks to go around, so we had to share.

o Finally, because of the large class size, part of many lessons included 'reading around the class' – there were too many of us to bounce ideas off each other in a small group, like they did in the agoras of Ancient Greece. Or, presumably even today, at Eton.

When I started this anecdote I hadn't realised what a huge amount of context would be needed to lead to a rather inconsequential denoument. But still.

Picture the scene. Endaf and I were sitting at two desks pushed together, with the textbook open between us, its spine above the gap. It was my turn to read out loud to the class. As I did so, almost imperceptibly, the book started to rise and fall, initially very slowly. At first I thought I was hallucinating. But the rise and fall increased in speed, the book beginning to look like a seagull taking off from the harbour. Endaf had pushed a ruler up between the desks. I continued reading manfully if distractedly, and the rest of the class, heads down over the set text, didn't seem to notice. I glanced at Endaf. He was, with elaborate innocence, looking intently at our shared book, seemingly unaware of the ruler rising and falling, with our textbook at one end and his fist at the other. I tried my best to continue, but in due course couldn't suppress a fit of the giggles. The rest of the class, looking up from its collective stupour, regarded me with astonishment. Brasso, ignoring my outburst, calmly asked somebody else to continue.

At the end of the lesson, as we were filing out, Brasso took me aside and said, 'I had no idea that Henry VII's fiscal policies were so funny.' I mumbled something and beat a retreat.

Brasso was already one of my heroes. His deadpan response confirmed it.

Endaf Emlyn – postscript

Several comments were forthcoming:

- Somebody confirmed that Brasso was a favourite among a wide selection of his pupils.

- A girl announced that Endaf had been her second boyfriend.

- Endaf's father had tried to teach another member of the group touch-typing. He failed, because the length of her nails prevented her fingers making contact with the keys.

- And there was just the briefest mention that Endaf's older sister was already at this time a famous harpist – Siân (or according to Wikipedia, 'Shân') Emlyn. Endaf played (violin) in the the Welsh National Youth Orchestra (together with John Cale), and went on, as I said before, to be a noted broadcaster, folk singer and cinematographter. What a talented family!

- A reposted photo of Endaf as a child led to a flurry of further comments from those who knew him at school. Concern was expressed that he seemed to have deleted his Facebook profile, leading to worry about his current state of health. As far as I know, he's still going strong.

- In addition to the film already mentioned (*Leaving Lenin*), a member of the group drew attention to another of his films (*Storms of August*) which was set in and around Pwllheli. IMDb notes the name among the films that Endaf directed, but with no further information.

Wili Kitch

A long time ago I mentioned that I'm a fan of Christine Evans, a poet who taught English at YRP. I'd left school by the time she arrived (though she did teach my younger brother), and I own copies of all her books of poetry and really rate them. I recently encountered a book of hers that I hadn't come across – not poetry, but a collection of essays describing her relationship with Ynys Enlli. It's called, simply, *Bardsey*. So I bought it.

No doubt I'll enjoy reading it, but that's not the point here. On the first page of the first essay she describes her arrival on the island. She'd just completed her first year's teaching at YRP, and had been invited to stay on Enlli by one of its residents, her YRP colleague Averilda Williams. The cookery teacher.

Yes, none other than Wili Kitch!

I don't know whether she owned the cottage on the island (she seems to have spent every summer there), whether she stayed in Pwllheli during term-time, or if not by what arrangements she was able to turn up at school each day throughout the year. In fact, it brought home to me that I knew absolutely nothing about her. But that first page sparked off three memories – my *only* memories – of Wili Kitch:

1. When I was in the third year, on a foul day of wind and torrential rain, I fell over on the school field, getting my trousers covered in mud. To be on that exposed field in such weather may seem insane, but at that time I was a smoker and (fellow nicotine-addicts will understand) I was on my way to smoker's corner at the top of Allt Bartu for a cigarette. Having slipped and come a cropper, I presented my filthy and bedraggled self to the teacher on duty (Bolwadin, I think) who sent me to see Wili Kitch. I fervently hoped to be sent home for a change of clothes. Instead she said briskly, 'We'll see what we can do. Take your trousers off,' and left the room. What? What! Not bloody likely! She was no doubt unsurprised to find on her return that I'd legged it, to spend the rest of the day clammy but with dignity intact. This was, I now suspect, an old hand's ploy on her part – I bet she'd used it many times before!

2. In my fifth year I suffered a nosebleed in Mol's 'O' Level

Biology class, caused entirely by my own stupidity and tendency to mess about. It involved a skeletal hand and the pretence that it was picking my nose. If you want to know the full story, check out my first book. Mol sent me to Wili Kitch, who was what we'd now call the school's dedicated first-aider. No doubt she administered the usual cures for nosebleeds recommended at the time. Pinching the bridge of the nose perhaps? A cold compress on the nape of the neck? Manipulation by the finger of birth-stangled babe, ditch-delivered by a drab? I don't know, but I have no memory of them. Perhaps it's just as well.

3. In form six Wili Kitch was invigilating one of my 'A' Level mock exams in the hall. Throughout the three hours of the exam she energetically and noisily cut up sheets of heavy cardboard with a large pair of scissors. I found this incredibly distracting. By the end of the exam I was indulging in blood-thirsty fantasies of running down to the front, seizing the scissors and plunging them into her heart. But I'm no fool. If it came to a physical confrontation between myself and Wili Kitch, I knew who'd have won, and it wouldn't have been me.

Wili Kitch was, then, peripheral to my secondary education. She was never my form teacher. I never took cookery or dressmaking (boys didn't in those days). I never encountered her when she was on duty. If it hadn't been that she invited Christine Evans to stay with her on Bardsey in the late 1960s, or that Christine Evans had written about it, I would never have given her a second thought.

So why am I writing this post?

- I've said elsewhere that I'm amazed at how little I knew about my teachers – even the ones I admired, like Brasso, Swift and Harry Hughes. So it's not surprising that I knew virtually nothing about teachers I hardly ever came across. Like Wili Kitch.

- My personal impression of her was of a powerfully-built woman, shortish in both stature and temper, a bit disheveled, brusque and no-nonsense. A woman who didn't suffer fools gladly.

- Bit of a mismatch with her given first name 'Averilda' (shortened to 'Rilda'). Google tells me that: 'When people hear the name 'Averilda' they perceive you as someone who is pleasing, stylish, diplomatic, gentle and graceful. Others may find you charming, with a certain sex-appeal.' Not I think a description of Wili Kitch that those who knew her would recognise.

- OK. What was she really like? I suspect that I'd have liked her. And I'm hoping to find out more about her as I work my way through Christine Evans's book. But until then I'd welcome impressions of her from others who were in school at around the same time, and who knew her a lot better than I did.

Wili Kitch – postscript

A. I've now finished reading the first section of *Bardsey*. This is how Wili Kitch comes out of it:

- 'Rilda' (as she is known throughout the book) seems to have been an unlikely cupid in Christine Evans's (or as she was then, Christine Doughty's) life. She introduced Christine to Bardsey by inviting her to stay at 'Nant'. As her week on the island was coming to an end, Rilda fell off a stool while clearing a high shelf, spraining her ankle. With the imminent arrival of a large church group (see below), she thankfully accepted Christine's offer to extend her stay to help out. And this extended stay allowed her relationship with Ernest, her husband-to-be, to deepen and flourish. Was the fall off the stool accident or subterfuge? Who knows.

- In between, Rilda appeared intermittently:

- o She sent Christine off to get the milk and butter from her very effective 'fridge' – an enamel bucket with lid secured by a large stone which sat in a fern-fringed rock basin into which water dripped from the well.
- o She sent her to the farm for butter and eggs.
- o She taught her how to make bread ('Lukewarm, I said,' as she tests the temperature of the mixture, 'That'll kill the yeast.')
- o She always seemed to be around in the background, working indefatigably. She was 'busy from early morning till night,' looking after her guests, cooking, scrubbing stairs, polishing windows, filling tins with fruitcakes and flapjacks, doing the washing (on Mondays) and hanging it out to dry.
- o She had also taken on the house next door ('Hendy') preparing it (see above) for the arrival of a large church party – cleaning it, fitting it out with beds and other furniture, making curtains, even whitewashing the outside privy.

- All in all, although never centre stage, she comes across as the energetic, practical, no-nonsense person that as a schoolboy I always assumed her to be.

B. As for the responses to my post, some of her pupils liked her, some didn't, which I'm sure can be said of all of us teachers. But with Wili Kitch, the former were very much in the ascendent:

- To those who continued an interest in cookery and dressmaking, she was an influential figure. But even her fans were not unaware that she could appear forbidding – 'Looks can be deceptive,' as one of her favourites says, rushing to her defence, 'she was a very caring lady'.

- And there can be no mistaking the affection with which she was remembered by many others:
  - o She would stay after school on Wednesdays until 6pm for additonal exam preparation.

- o She consoled a girl whose father had died by giving her and her sister cups of tea during break.
- o She trusted pupils to go into town to get materials for lessons, and invited favoured students to stay with her on Enlli.
- o She brought her spaniel ('Chaddy') to school and allowed children to walk her on the Garn during lunchtimes.

- Her dress-sense left its mark – 'big brown skirt, cream ankle socks folded over above sensible brown lace-up shoes.' And at times a school blazer with YB on it (Ysgol Botwnnog?).

- One memory, possibly apocryphal, was of her washing hanging on a line above the domestic-science-room Aga.

- Some of her favourite sayings were quoted:
  - o 'You may cut' (when satisfied with patterns laid on cloth).
  - o 'Where do the eggshells go?' Response: 'Straight in the bin Miss.'
  - o 'Serve on a doily on a plate, bring a tin to carry them home.'

- And a great deal of biographical information was volunteered:
  - o She was born in 1902, the daughter of the Rev. William Willams, rector of Llangwnnadl.
  - o She taught at YRP from the early 1930s, transferred to Glan-y-Môr for her final year, and retired in 1970.
  - o During term-time she lived in Llangwnnadl and got to Pwllheli on the Number 8 bus. During holidays (at least during the summer) she stayed on Enlli.
  - o At some point she was housekeeper to the Archdeacon of Meirionnydd in Llanelltyd near Dolgellau.
  - o She died in 1976 and is buried in Llangwnnadl

churchyard. The group member who reported this included a photo of her gravestone.

On the other hand, she was certainly formidable, so there were negative comments:

- One of her charges would, at the beginning of term, pray for bad weather so that Wili Kitch would be stuck on Bardsey, unable to get to school.

- Another was so frightened of her that she deliberately opted to have her violin lessons at the time she should have been in needlework classes.

- The consensus seems to be that she had favourites (even the favourites agree on this) who received better treatment than those less blessed.

- An interesting comment from one member of the group saw the two teachers as something of an odd couple: 'She [Wili Kitch] was quite formidable, yet my strongest memories were of her and Miss Doughty being an unlikely pair, as the latter was very modern by comparison.'

I know what she means – the idealistic and sensitive young ingénue, the practical old hand who took her under her wing.

But from the evidence of Bardsey, and from all I've learned about Christine Evans from her poetry, they certainly shared a capacity for hard work and a devotion to Enlli and Llŷn.

Gender at YRP

My recent post about Wili Kitch, together with the comments that it provoked, ran to over 1,700 words. Why did I spend so much time writing about a member of staff who never taught me, with whom I had virtually no contact during my secondary education, and whose influence on me was negligible? The answer occurred to me as I read the comments. They were almost all from girls. Of course they were – Wili Kitch taught cookery and dressmaking and nothing else, so she only ever came into daily contact with girls. And this took me back to a criticism that was made of my first book – that the picture it painted of life in Pwllheli was entirely from a boy's perspective. I'd responded, indignantly, that I couldn't help that, since I was a boy. But here, in my second book, I saw an opportunity, at least to a small extent, to put this right by giving several pages over to the one teacher at YRP whose dealings were entirely with girls.

This led me to give some thought not only to gender but to gender balance at YRP.

- As far as I remember, the school had some 450 pupils. Assuming that the gender balance must have been 50/50 (around 225 of each), and among staff something similar, I took out my panoramic photo of the staff and pupils of YRP 1961–62, and counted the teachers – eighteen men, seven women. Quite an imbalance. And no, I didn't count the number of boys and girls as well – the photo's a metre long, the kids stand and sit between four and seven ranks deep. Be reasonable.

- This led me to further memories of the men's and women's staffrooms. They were at either end of the upstairs corridor – as far apart as they could be while staying within the school. Were the planners afraid that they would fraternise? Or breed?

- My memories of waiting at the door of the two staffrooms could not have been different:

  o From the open door of the women's staffroom I could see that the room was clean, full of sunlight and pastel colours, with a tablecloth held in place by a large vase of fresh flowers on a big central table. I can't be sure, but I might even have glimpsed a permanent rainbow in one corner, and unicorns grazing peacefully on sunlit uplands.

  o From the door of the men's staffroom all I could see was a solid wall of tobacco smoke. The roar – of shouted conversation, of banter and laughter – was deafening. Again I can't be sure, but I think I caught glimpses of cloven hooves and forked tails, perhaps devils shoveling fuel into the maw of gigantic infernal ovens, roasting those who'd sinned, or at least had failed to hand in their homework on time.

- Up till now I thought that these two experiences simply reflected stereotyped gender differences. But considering that the two rooms were the same size, and that the men's staffroom housed eighteen (or rather seventeen – Boss had his own office) men while the women's staffroom catered for seven women, then perhaps I was being a bit harsh on the men.

Nah! The women were civilized, fragrant. The men – weren't.

Gender at YRP – postscript

Two strands of discussion emerged from the comments to my post about gender at YRP, one directly relevant, the other not so much, but interesting:

- Several people corroborated my memories of the two staffrooms – especially the dense fug in the men's. The question was posed – what happened to male staff who didn't smoke – did they (as everybody did before the ban on smoking in public places) just put up with it? Resigned themselves to an early death which was not their fault? One teacher (and one not normally thought of as being in the heroic mould) obviously stood his ground and made a stand. Bono. A non-smoker, he occupied his own little one-man smoke-free staff annex – next to the men's staffroom.

- Several other comments, though not directly relevant to gender differences, seemed to point to how things were earlier in the twentieth century:
  - o Most of the teachers (and I can bear this out) wore graduates' gowns. The only two in the panoramic

photograph (see above) who didn't wear gowns were Jack Wood and Wili Kitch – boys and girls crafts. Presumably not graduates. But it was the condition of these gowns that was the issue – they were, apparently, in a dreadful state of repair. Now I don't wish to perpetuate gender stereotypes, but it has to be said that it was a female ex-pupil who raised the matter. And it wasn't, as you might expect, to deplore the state of male teachers' gowns as compared to those of the women – they were all, apparently, execrable! So Bethan Ogwen was castigated for a gown that looked as if it had been run over by the groundsman's mower while she was practising her hockey, while Brasso looked askance at the no doubt kindly offer from that female pupil to try to repair his dilapidated gown. I'm sure it's to his credit that he really hadn't noticed any shortcoming in his attire – a man after my own heart. The member (indeed the founder) of the group who put forward these criticisms of the staff's academic garb even went so far as to wonder whether there was an unofficial, even subversive, competition among staff to see who could wear the most disreputable dress without being called to the head's office for (appropriately) a dressing down. I really – I mean really – hope that there was. I fondly imagine a prize being awarded on speech day to the teacher whose gown was the most threadbare, most disgraceful, most scandalous!

o A further comment pointed out that Seu didn't wear an academic gown either. I checked the photo, and sure enough it was true. It made me think. My feeling was that Seu arrived in teaching by a route other than the normal one through university. In 'A' Level Economics he once said that he learned all he knew about the subject from the financial pages of the *Manchester Guardian*. Which brought further memories of him, once a week, walking down into town to carry out his duties as a JP, always with copy of the *Guardian* newspaper tucked under his arm. I had a lot of time for Seu, and I've read the *Guardian* ever since.

o It was pointed out (with a degree of disbelief) that the women's staff room was actually, within the school, widely referred to as 'the mistresses room'. Make of that what you will.

o A further indication of how things used to be came in the leaving speech of a popular member of staff – Maldwyn – who mentioned, with some wistfulness, that earlier in his career teachers addressed each other by title and surname – Mister this or Miss that or Mrs the other. By the time of his retirement, though, it was all chummy first names. Except for Boss, who was still universally addressed as, 'Mr Hughes'. Not by us kids, I'd have to admit.

Fighting

Relationships, of course, are not necessarily positive or life affirming.

When writing about Pwllheli, I've avoided mentioning something that was, in my memory, ever-present – as I'm sure it was (and probably is) in every small town in the world. An air of violence. Specifically, fighting. I've avoided talking about it for a simple reason – it worried me then, it still does, and I wasn't very good at it. But fights certainly qualify as relationships.

Within groups of us, even within the town as a whole, there was an accepted order of who were the hard men, who could beat whom, which was rarely voiced or contested. When it *was* successfully challenged, it led to a rearrangement of the hierarchy, what sociologists would call a paradigm shift. I remember two such challenges – one by Mop, the other by Mike Bowey, both in Brexo. I can't remember who they challenged, but I was overwhelmed with admiration. I could feel the paradigm shift happening as I watched.

And this was only within Pwllheli itself. At dances (for example in the Legion in Pwllheli or at Cricieth's Memorial Hall), groups of lads from towns and villages all over Llŷn contributed to a really explosive mix. You could smell the brew of violence and testosterone in the air.

I still find this difficult to write about, over half a century later. But I'll try:

- First – 'loms'. This was the word we Pwllheli sophisticates would use to describe lads from the villages and the farms. They were Welsh-speaking (often very uncomfortable in English), and, to our shame, we looked down on them. In my case at least, this was entirely because I was terrified of them. They were often immensely strong, from doing all sorts of tough work that would have killed me, and they had nothing but contempt for us – as we liked to think of ourselves – city slickers. On the bright side, they only came into Pwllheli on Wednesdays and Saturdays. And usually had to catch the bus back to their farms and villages at ten o'clock.

- Next – among friends. I am a gentle soul with not a pugnacious bone in my body. Or so I like to think. Yet, the odd thing is that, looking back, I can't remember any of my friends getting involved in fights except myself and Ginge. And the one fight that I remember Ginge getting involved in was with me. Go figure.

- Finally, to cut to the embarrassing chase, my fights included the following:
    o With an English lad as we came off the Garn. I don't know how it started (probably me showing off), it became a scuffle, and we both retreated with honours even.

o As I was coming up to 'O' Levels, in Market Square, we were messing about. David Hambling (related to Garnett? Brian? Both? I can't remember), who worked in the chip shop, suddenly punched me full in the face. I fell to the floor, shot up incandescent with indignation, and he punched me again. My lip was split and there was blood everywhere. I had no idea what had happened, or why. A number of things have since occurred to me over the years:

§ I was humiliated at the time. But on reflection, he was a full-grown man, with powerful shoulders, who'd felled a nine-stone youth whom a light breeze could have blown away.

§ I really didn't want to tell people what had happened. Partly, of course, because I was really (I mean, *really*) embarrassed. But also because I couldn't see my father picking up the cudgels on my behalf. I could hear his outraged voice. 'Brawling in the street? What were you thinking?' So I made up a story about swinging from trees next to the harbour as I was hauled off to have a stitch put into my lip by Doctor Charles.

§ I did OK in the 'O' Level exams a few weeks later. So no harm done.

• The only fight I ever won was against Ginge. I have no memory of what it was about, but it happened in the sixth form as we came in off the field onto the slope in front of the woodwork room. It took about ten seconds, but it was excruciatingly public. Ginge did me the honour of telling somebody, after the fact, that he'd never been hit so often, so hard, so quickly. What a gentleman – paying respects to what I like to call his vanquisher! I think he was just being polite. We were best mates within minutes.

• Final story. Robin (who later ran the Castle pub) sat in

Brexo, and patronisingly told me to watch my step (I have no memory of what about). I told him to 'F-off'. We agreed to walk out and settle our differences behind the Palladium. With an audience of Brexo customers (all of them) who'd followed us out, we began to grapple. I 'dropped a head on him' (quite proud of that at the time), but then he seized my tie and throttled me into submission. I was what – sixteen? I was wearing a tie! At the weekend! In the afternoon! Those days are gone. Dil, I seem to remember, thought the whole thing hilarious!

So that's it. I'm glad I've got that off my chest!

Fighting – postscript

Given that I'd felt edgy about raising the question of violence and fighting in '50s and '60s Pwllheli, but that to ignore it would falsify the picture of our lives that I was trying to create, I was reassured by the varied responses:

- One group member summed up the perplexity admirably. 'Yes, there was a curious slight undercurrent of generally petty mild violence underpinning our largely idyllic-ish growing up.' Spot on, and beautifully put!

- I was startled to discover that my gentle younger brother had been involved in 'a scrap' at school. He and his adversary had quickly become the focus of 'a human arena of bottle-green-jacketed boys' chanting 'Fight. Fight. Fight!' Shortly afterwards, he was summoned to the head ER's office, not to be reprimanded, as he expected, but to be told he was being 'promoted' to a higher stream. And he'd even arranged his hair to cover his black eye!

- Someone else referred to a fight with another boy into which they had been 'goaded', and which still, a lifetime later, provoked real regret. Again beautifully put. 'It remains a heaviness.'

- Finally, a comment that 'Everyone studiously avoids mentioning bullying' led me to think that this might be because, in adulthood, both the bullies (with reason) and the bullied (for no reason at all) feel ashamed.

The responses to my post on fighting were accompanied by a wonderful painting of 'Cwffio ar y maes' on fair days in Cricieth. Some things never change! It really put the whole thing in perspective.

'If I fell'

In most families, I suspect, there's a song that has a special part to play in that family's history, a special place in its heart. In mine, it was 'If I Fell' by the Beatles, and I associate it most strongly with my older brother Jeff and later with my daughter Catherine. It was written in February 1964 (no, I don't remember. I looked it up) when I was seventeen and just beginning my revision for 'A' Levels.

I first heard it when The Beatles sang it live on telly, and they made a complete hash of the harmonies. But I could tell right away that it was a beautiful song. The words were irrelevant, the harmonies were potentially stunning.

A bit of background. My brother Jeff and I, in our different ways, were Beatles fans. As we got older, our preferences among the four mopheads (I know, I know) became established. And as they say, opposites attract. Jeff was an iconoclast, a bit of a rebel, a follower of the 'bugger-what-other-people-think' school of thought. So he plumped for Paul McCartney, the archetypal nice-guy people-pleaser. My favourite was (and still is) John Lennon, the damaged, sarcastic adherent of the 'couldn't-give-a-damn' approach to life. I, needless to say, wouldn't say boo to a goose. I'm sure that, if I'd ever met them, I would have loved Paul, hated John.

So when Jeff and I first sang 'If I fell' (in a pub, of course, late at night) it was inevitable that I would sing Lennon's low harmony and Jeff would sing McCartney's high melody. We didn't have to discuss it, we didn't have to check if we knew the lyrics. It just happened.

From then on, we sang 'If I fell' virtually every time we found ourselves drinking together in a pub. Or after last orders, as we walked home. We even, years later and after midnight, sang it in the quadrangle of Magdalen College Oxford, lying on the grass with Jeff's son Siôn who we were visiting. Until somebody opened a window and yelled at us to shut the fuck up. In a posh accent. We sang it at the karaoke at my daughter's wedding, with Catherine joining in as guest vocalist. To, I'm sure I remember, considerable applause. Catherine even, later in life, gave me an audiograph of the song as a birthday present.

Long after Jeff died, and still missing him, I suggested that Catherine, no mean singer herself (I still get goosebumps remembering her rendition, with a friend, of 'She's Leaving Home' at a school concert), or her husband Matt (who caused a world-wide internet sensation as the 'bearded hottie' singing the lead in a clip of his choir winding down after rehearsals in their local pub), might want to take Jeff's part. They flatly refused. They felt that 'If I fell' was special to me and Jeff, and that replacing him would be sacrilege.

A common – almost cliché – question on celebrity interviews is, 'What song would you like played at your funeral?' At mine, no question.

The birdie song.

'If I fell' – postscript

- This is the sort of clever Dick joke to which I'm unfortunately prone. At my funeral, the song I want played is, of course, 'If I Fell', sung by Lennon and McCartney. But since Lennon's dead, sung by me and Jeff. But since Jeff's dead... oh, never mind. (PS. If you read this Paul and we're both still alive, I'd love to give it a go!)

- If there's a Plan B in the family song stakes, I'd have

to name 'Hey Joe'. I have so many happy memories of singing it during after-pub sessions, with my son Dan playing the chords and the central guitar riff that I was never able to master. If I have a doubt, it's because I remember a recording of Jimi Hendrix breaking off half-way through it, muttering 'Enough of this shit', and diving into something else. Oh, and the fact that it's about the murder of a woman by a man.

Secondary school epiphanies

Relationships are usually with people, but they can also be with subjects. It wasn't until long after I'd left YRP that I began to consider my relationships with the school subjects I'd studied. Given that I spent seven years of my life at YRP, it's remarkable how little I remember of what I was supposed to have learnt. Yet certain things did stick. I've called them epiphanies (definition: 'A moment of sudden revelation.'). Pretentious, or what!

Biology

Up to 'O' Level, my great love was Biology. Not because my teachers – Mol and Juicy – were, though very nice, particularly charismatic, but because I just loved the subject. Whatever we studied, I didn't even have to learn it: I seemed to know it already. So, for example, all the main bones of the skeleton I knew without thinking. In fact, the only part of 'O' Level Biology I never got to grips with was digestion, and all those enzymes. Even so, today when I've got indigestion, I'll try to generate as much spit as I can and swallow it – the ptyalin helps, I seem to remember. Though I can appreciate that that's probably too much information.

I would have loved to have done Biology to 'A' Level, but at YRP, if you wanted to do Botany and Zoology, you had to do Chemistry. And I hated Chemistry. I remember Mol's disappointment when he heard that I was going to do English, History and Economics. But looking at Swift, Brasso, Harry and even Seu, it was no contest. I knew who I wanted to be like.

My first biological epiphany was caused by primroses. They seemed to be so intricate, so well designed, that it was inconceivable that their development was random, even over however many billions of years that Darwin suggested.

Let me explain. There are two sorts of primroses: pin-eyed, and thrum-eyed.

Look at a primrose:

- If, at the centre of the petals, there's a clearcut dot, it's a pin-eyed primrose. That dot is the tip of the stigma, joined by the style to the ovary at the base of the petals, waiting to be fertilised by, hopefully, pollen from a different plant. Its own pollen is created by a cluster of stamens which is hidden half-way down the trumpet of the flower.

- If, at the centre of the petals, there's a slightly confused group of powdery things, that means that it's a thrum-eyed primrose. The thrum (so-called because they look like the frayed end of a piece of weaving – the thrum) is a cluster of stamens, waiting to give up their pollen. This time it's the *stigma* that is hidden half-way down the trumpet of the flower.

So (stay with me) a bee lands on a thrum-eyed primrose and reaches its tongue down into the trumpet of the flower to get at the nectar at the base of the ovary. It picks up pollen from the stamens on its forehead. Then, when it flies off to a pin-eyed primrose, it deposits the pollen from its forehead onto the stigma, thus fertilising the flower, while picking up pollen on its tongue from the stamens half-way down the trumpet. Then off to the next thrum-eyed primrose, and off it goes again. God exists, and is the architect of everything in the universe. The universe is a clock, God the clockmaker.

I became a creationist.

But then we studied the humble groundsel plant. Mol explained how its roots drew sustenance from the soil, how its leaves created energy from the sun, how its petals attracted insects to fertilize its ovaries, to generate seeds to ensure that a new plant would grow to replace the old one. And the new plant would go through the same sequence, to create yet another groundsel plant. And on, throughout eternity. And on. And on.

Why? To what end? For what purpose?

It didn't take long for me to extend all that to humanity. Everything in the human body is designed to ensure the survival of the species. The legs to allow it to hunt for food, run away from predators, or chase a mate. It's digestion to convert food into energy to fuel these activities. Its lungs to oxygenate the blood, to feed the cells and remove impurities. Its eyes to look for food (or a mate, or a predator), its ears to listen out for danger or hear a mating call. Its brain to coordinate all of this. And above all, the testes to create the sperm, the ovaries to generate the eggs, and the whole palaver – of sexual attraction, of maternal instinct, of fighting off threats, of love songs and romcoms – all to ensure that egg and sperm meet, to create another human being, to ensure the survival of the species. Just like the groundsel plant.

Whether you're a groundsel plant or Albert Einstein, everything is designed to support the blind drive to continue the species.

Why? To what end? For what purpose?

A host of religions developed to try to answer those questions. But they cut no ice with me.

I became an atheist.

Looking back, I'm amazed that I ever managed to get a girlfriend.

English

1. Wordsworth's poems about the beauty of the Lake District, and its influence on him when he was growing up, made me look at Llŷn in a new light.

2. Gerard Manley Hopkins was clearly one of Swift's favourite poets, and that was good enough for me. We didn't actually study any of his poems, but Swift often quoted from him, and we did read 'The Windhover' and 'Pied Beauty' in class. I've read Hopkins since, though not often. He's *really* difficult!

Physics

John Maurice used to take the mickey out of Dick Ed's physics teaching by chanting out the passage in the textbook that Dick was dictating to the class, only a split-second ahead. OK, dictating what's already in the textbook does seem a bit pointless. Yet I was impressed by how Physics explained so much useful stuff:

1. That thermostats use a bimetallic strip to keep things (fridge, central heating etc.) at a constant temperature.

2. That an electric bell uses a spring and the fact that passing current through a wire that's wrapped around a piece of iron magnetises the iron.

Physics might be difficult, but at least it was *useful*!

Welsh

My epiphanies in Welsh were threefold, one general, one specific, one linguistic:

1. In general, I was blown away by how beautiful the language is. I could get pleasure in reading it aloud (when there was nobody else around, of course), even when I hardly understood a word. It also introduced me to difference between second person singular (friendly and/

or overfamiliar) and the second person plural (formal, respectful), a difference to be found in most European languages, but which has atrophied in English. The difference was impressed upon me when I addressed our teacher Mair as *ti* instead of *chi*. The whole class laughed. You don't forget a lesson like that.

2. Specifically, I remember writing a piece for Mair about how worries (exams, for example) loom like dark clouds ahead of you, that they become more and more threatening as they approach, but then pass over you and recede into the past. The sun comes out, and you enjoy blue skies again – until the next cloud forms. She was very complimentary, and I was cock-a-hoop. I'd explained quite an abstract idea. In Welsh!

3. As for linguistics (or do I mean semantics), I need to go back to Miss Jones's class at Penlleiniau. We had a Welsh-language book which included a copy of *The Laughing Cavalier* by Frans Hals. By the time I'd finished with it, his face had been erased. That's that of the 'Laughing Cavalier', not Frans Hals. It wasn't because I was a natural vandal, a defacer of books, but because my command of Welsh fell far short of perfection. The caption of the picture told the reader to study (*craffu*) the face of the cavalier. I read it as *crafu* – scratch. So I did. Just think – I was *that* close to inventing the scratch card!

History

Again, general and specific:

1. Generally, I appreciated that history, like life, deals with difficult questions, with no easy answers. That it demands evidence for opinions. That it develops judgement.

2. More specifically, I discovered that I preferred quiet, unshowy competence (Henry VII, Clement Attlee) to colourful showmanship (Henry VIII, Boris Johnson).

Maths

I was good at Maths. I got good marks. I even won the school 'O' Level Maths prize. Yet I was really rubbish at it. In Maths, I was constantly turning around to ask Nan and Kiff how to do things. They were very patient. But nothing could disguise the fact that they understood Maths, and I didn't. I could kind of see the point of Geometry and Trigonometry (marking out football pitches, for example, or measuring a room for a new carpet), but not Algebra.

I have one example which I've been banging on about for the last sixty years. Another came late in life:

1.   Quadratic equations. By the time I finished 'O' Levels, I could solve quadratic equations in three ways: one involving brackets (!), one with a formula (which I can still quote) and one by drawing graphs. But I have no idea what quadratic equations are, or what they're for. I Googled quadratic equations. I'm still none the wiser.

2.   But I did eventually see the point of Algebra. It is, as I understand it, like arithmetic (which is obviously useful, to stop your older brother conning you out of your pocket money) but is much more generally valuable. Instead of dealing with specific numbers, it deals with boxes (like x, or y) into which you can put any numbers you like, and which therefore create a formula which you can use in lots of different situations.

Chemistry

Chemistry was an epiphany-free zone. You added chemical A to chemical B, it effervesced, and resulted in compound C. We might just as well have been adding vinegar to fish and chips and describing the outcome. I bear no ill will towards Chemistry. Except that it stopped me doing Biology and Zoology at 'A' Level. Correction – I'll never forgive Chemistry.

Geography

Driving through Eryri with my family, we came to the head of a majestic valley. My teenage son told us that it was U-shaped, explained that it was formed by glaciers, and pointed out some of its essential features. How did he know, I enquired? Surely he couldn't remember the Ice Age? GCSE Geography, he said.

It was then that I realised that there were two types of Geography – human and physical. All we'd done up to the third year was human geography, which I remembered as lists of stuff produced by lists of countries. That's why I dropped Geography for 'O' Level. If I'd known that there was all this scientific theory that would explain so much of the landscapes around me, I'm sure I'd have at least considered it. A minor epiphany, then, but far too late to influence my life.

Secondary school epiphanies – postscript

1. Comments brought home to me, a one-time secondary school timetabler, how decisions made, perhaps at home sitting in ones underpants (too much information), or at a pub table, or while watching telly, or while being told off for getting ones planners out on Christmas day, could affect the future lives of hundreds of schoolchildren. Including, now I think about it, myself. But it wasn't (his daughter tells me) Maldwyn's fault. Even though he did the timetabling at YRP. He was just following orders. The broad outlines were decided by the head.

2. Ptyalin stops working when it enters the stomach. A lifetime swallowing my own spit, it turns out, was so much wasted effort. Though on reflection, I'd rather swallow my own spit than somebody else's. Which reminds me of a joke about the spittoon in a Western saloon. Oh, never mind.

3. John Maurice's brother confirmed that that was just the sort of thing that John would have done. John Maurice was one of nature's comedians.

4. My account of pin-eyed and thrum-eyed primroses was characterised by one commentator, who shall remain nameless (oh, alright, Tony Pierce), as their sex life. Primroses! Some people's minds are like sewers.

Dewi Sant

Finally, somebody with whom most people in Pwllheli – indeed, most people in Wales – had a relationship. He affected us all, even if we didn't know it, or know him personally. Our patron saint Dewi Sant – St David.

At my primary school (Penlleiniau), we used to have a half-day's holiday on March first – Dydd Gŵyl Dewi Sant. We'd spend the morning hearing about his life and doing other St David-related things, though I can't remember what – drawing daffodils, perhaps, or designing greetings cards, or putting on little plays. Then at lunchtime we'd be sent home.

OK, we didn't know St David as such. There's quite a stretch of time between his fifth and our twenty-first centuries. Surely, though, the patron saint of a country both helps to mould that country's character, and also reflects its favoured attitudes and beliefs, the characteristics it values.

So, what was our patron saint like? Even as a small boy, I can remember being a bit underwhelmed by St David. Take his most memorable miracle. While addressing a crowd, people at the back complained that they couldn't hear or see him properly. So he put a cloth down on the ground, and when he'd done so, a small hillock grew up beneath it, upon which he stood and completed his sermon. Presumably those at the back were grateful, but as miracles go it was a bit, well, modest. A small hillock in what is, let's face it, a pretty mountainous country.

I wondered how the miracles of other UK patron saints compared:

- St George killed a dragon.

- St Patrick cast out snakes from Ireland, which to this day remains a snake-free zone.
- St Andrew, a really big-hitter, not only did miracles all over Europe (Georgia, Cyprus, Malta, Romania, Spain, even Scotland), but was one of Jesus's senior management team. He was also brother of Simon Peter, the rock upon which Christianity was built. An impressive CV.

So next I looked at how they'd lived, and how they died:

- St George was a swashbuckling soldier, who was eventually beheaded for his faith.
- St Andrew spread Christianity all over Europe, and was crucified on an X-shaped cross (at his own request – he didn't want to upstage his boss).
- St Patrick's style was closer to that of St David in that he concentrated on spreading the word in his own country, though had to be satisfied with sharing the patron saint honours with Brigid of Kildare and Columba. Like St David he also seems to have died of natural causes.
- And St David? He did his job – setting up churches. He didn't moonlight as a dragon-slayer, or hobnob with Jesus and St Peter, or swan around banishing snakes. His final exhortation to his flock was, 'Do the little things in life,' and he died, a few days later, of old age. A modest man.

Finally, St David was born and bred in the country of which he became patron saint, something that can't be said of any of the others:

- St George was a Greek, born in what is today Turkey.
- St Andrew was Galilean.
- St Patrick was from the north of Britain – either northern England or Scotland. He only ended up in Ireland after being kidnapped by pirates.

So, since those far off days of being sent home down Salem Terrace on the first of March, feeling a bit embarrassed

111

by my patron saint, I've revised my opinion. Saint David was everything I've come to admire in my heroes – modest, competent, unflashy, and with his heart very much in the right place.

A patron saint to be proud of. Let's hear it for Dewi Sant!

Dewi Sant – postscript

- Many of the comments (not hugely respectful, I have to say) centred around one of the numerous stories about St David – that he lived entirely on water and leeks.
  - o He was known, apparently, as 'watery Dave'.
  - o There was some speculation as to what effect such a diet might have had on his saintly odour.
  - o Somebody pointed out that the more water you drink, the more leaks you'd need. Arf, arf.
  - o Somebody else wanted to know if he ate daffodils for pudding.

- I wasn't the only one to notice that St David's most famous miracle – the creation of a small hillock (to improve the gig experience of his fans) in a land famous for its mountains, lacked impact. No less a figure than the distinguished Welsh historian John Davies described it in his *A History of Wales* as a 'most superfluous miracle'.

- There was agreement, too, that St David's character and that of the Welsh in general were highly compatible: 'No razzmatazz, everything done in a quiet, civilized manner. Typically Welsh, low key and with stealth.'

- It was even reported that there is a claim that St Patrick himself may have been Welsh. I wouldn't, though, care to repeat that in an Irish bar.

CHAPTER 4

Miscellaneous

FINALLY, A COUPLE of memories that weren't about things we did, nor places we went, nor people we knew or had relationships with, but were worth keeping in. I couldn't fit them in anywhere else, so I've collected them under that perennially useful heading: 'miscellaneous'.

Suspender belts

Younger members of the group will probably have no idea what a suspender belt is or was. But its shortcomings led to a recurring problem for my mother. When getting ready to go out, she would often plaintively ask if anybody had a sixpenny piece. This (again for younger members of the group) was a small silver coin, worth 2.5p. She needed it, not to spend but to fix that said item of feminine clothing – the suspender belt. It was a complicated arrangement of cloth, rubber and metal designed to keep stockings up. The sixpence was to replace a button which had come off, and which would be pushed into the top of the stocking, then slid into a sort of bracket which was attached to the suspender belt. As an explanation, that's the best I can do. These (the suspender belt and stockings) were reputed to be highly arousing to a certain age and class of men, though I've never been able to see it myself. Fashion note – suspender belts largely disappeared (at least from polite society) with the invention of the mini-skirt and the knock-on development of tights.

God exists

In our house in Llŷn Street, we had a pear tree in the back garden, just outside the scullery, to which my brother and I had tied a rope. Under the tree, for a while, we had a tin bath full of water in which our pet frog lived. OK, not so much a pet, more a captive. One Sunday, waiting to go to church, I was swinging above the tin bath. Like, I fondly imagined, Tarzan above a lagoon. Except that, rather than a loin cloth, I was wearing my Sunday best. And rather than a jungle vine, I was swinging on an old piece of rope. The rope broke, I fell into the bath, our frog (I hope) hopped it, and, not having any other clothes suitable for the worship of the Lord, I was told to repair to my attic bedroom to consider the error of my ways. I put on my pyjamas and sat out my disgrace lying on my bed reading, or finishing my model aeroplane at the big table under the eaves. I even took advantage of the empty house by having a crafty smoke out of my bedroom window, watching the rest of the family going off to church down Llŷn Street.

There is a God, I thought.

Conclusion

So there you have it – a mass of stories about life in north Wales in the 1950s and '60s, to add to the ones I included in my first book (still widely available etc…)

When I left Pwllheli to go to university, like many eighteen year olds I gave little thought to the future. The totality of my ambition was to survive being away from home, to make new friends, to drink as much as I could, and avoid being kicked out of college. But, with the benefit of hindsight, I realise that I was stomach-churningly terrified, but also delighted to be going out into the world, to begin life as a grown-up.

Part Two

Exile

My train pulled out of Pwllheli station in a cloud of steam. I had a smile on my face, a song in my heart and razor-winged butterflies in the pit of my stomach. Life away from Pwllheli. Growing up. I didn't know it at the time, but I would never live full-time in Wales again.

Jump forward a half-century. Revisiting childhood is a great pleasure in itself – hence the many 'nostalgia' FB groups, websites and books. But as I was enjoying looking back over my first eighteen years on this planet, I started thinking about my Welshness, and how this had affected me during the rest of my life in England. So step-by-step, mentally, I walked my way through my life from then to now. And at first saw Wales fading away before my very eyes.

CHAPTER 5

A Welshman in London

NOT A WELSHMAN, exactly – a Welsh *youth* perhaps. I could even live with 'Welsh bloke,' or 'Welsh lad'. I just didn't feel grown-up enough to be called a *man*. I still don't, and I'm seventy-seven.

In my first year

It was October 1964. I knew nothing about my destination (the London School of Economics) but I'd liked the picture in the student handbook they'd sent me – an empty lecture theatre with the caption 'The inaugural meeting of the Apathy Society'.

I was the first in my family to go to university (apart from cousin Christine, but she was far away in south Wales). It being London, and England, I expected everybody to be posh. I was surprised, as the train slid into Euston Station, to see ordinary people working on the railway lines, at the station, everywhere really. Just like at home. Not a monocle or top hat in sight. Who knew?

I expected, too, that all my fellow students would be posh, and southern. Again, not so. They were from Liverpool, Chesterfield, Leicester, Stoke-on-Trent. The furthest south was High Wycombe. Wherever that is. And they were from working-class backgrounds. Not one of them privately educated or noticeably upper crust.

In what I learned to call my freshman year, as never before in my life I *felt* Welsh:

- The first consequence was immediate, and brutal. Having fondly imagined as I grew up in Pwllheli that my accent was perfect received pronunciation as heard on the BBC, I found that in fact nobody in London understood anything I said. Not a word. They would beg my pardon several times and finally nod vaguely and look away, clearly still none the wiser. (Things, incidentally, were no better three years later. My wife insists that when I asked her to marry me, she agreed only because she didn't know what I'd said. 'Will you carry me?' perhaps. Seems reasonable – I'd had a few.

- Then there was the commute. Travelling by train from Pwllheli to London, the charge for luggage ('hold' luggage, as it would be today with non-budget airlines) was, as long as you had a ticket for the whole journey, minimal. So, since my ticket was booked from Pwllheli to Euston, for a nominal charge my trunk (remember those?) was collected from our house in Llŷn Street and delivered to my hall of residence in Bloomsbury. Efficient, effective, and so so easy. Don't believe those who claim that nationalised British Rail was inefficient.

When I tried to book the return trip at the end of my first term, there was a snag. Dr Beeching had shut the line between Afon Wen and Caernarfon weeks before I wanted to use it. I felt victimised, though to be fair he shut railway lines all over the country. So, arriving in Euston with my trunk, to secure its, and my, passage, I was asked to pay an eye-watering amount of money because there was now no continuous route between Euston and Pwllheli. I had to go from Paddington.

I loaded my trunk into a taxi, crossed London from one station to the other, and had to travel through darkest mid Wales and up the coast on the Cambrian Coast Express. And, despite its name, don't imagine *Mallard* or the *Flying*

Scotsman – it was a little engine with two carriages. As we approached Llŷn, the guard came through, asking each passenger where they wanted to get off.

'Pwllheli', I said.

'We're stopping there!' he replied with a grin.

Pwllheli's the terminus. The joke was repeated every time I went home for the next three years.

- It was handy having a father who was a keen amateur potter. My first year in London was spent in my college's hall of residence ('Passfield') on the edge of Bloomsbury. Each evening tea and coffee was served in the common room, with students being limited to one cup. So I wrote to Dad, explained the problem, and asked him to make me a very large mug. His response held a full pint, and even had my name on the front, to stop it being nicked.

- After a sticky start at LSE, and excruciating homesickness, I made friends and, towards the end of our first year, a group of us decided to buy an old van and drive to Istanbul. As you do. We planned a route, bought the van, and tried to think of ways to finance the trip. My contribution was to apply to a charity set up (I think) to encourage young Welsh people to travel, then offer advice to the Welsh Tourist Board. Our MP Goronwy Roberts recommended me. I filled in a grant application and was called for interview somewhere on Oxford Street.

The interviewer was kind. He mildly probed the intentions of our 'Black Sea Expedition'. I did my best. But at the end of the interview he said, gently, 'So really, you're just going on holiday?' And honestly, I couldn't disagree.

I didn't get the grant.

On the bright side, my mates did little better. Our total sponsorship amounted to a box of Oxo Cubes.

- I played rugby for London University. This is not as impressive as it sounds. Let me explain. London University was made up of lots of different, and scattered, colleges.

Each college had its own rugby team, but there was also a team who represented the university's combined student organisation, the University of London Union. Anybody who had any ability in rugby played for their college. The ULU team was, therefore (and I apologise to any members of the team who might, half a century later, be reading this) a ragbag of misfits and ne'er-do-wells who had no hope of getting into any of their college teams. I was asked if I wanted to play for them, on the grounds that I was Welsh. Flattered, I agreed and turned out on a sports ground somewhere in south London. I played the full eighty minutes. ULU hadn't been able to summon up a full team, so I ended up playing on both wings. I made no spectacular runs. I tackled nobody. I scored no tries. Any fears I may have provoked in the opposition by my being Welsh proved totally unfounded. Since I was both wings, I spent the whole match zig-zagging from one touchline to the other, putting the ball into lineouts. This was my only function. By the final whistle, I was so knackered that I could barely untie my boots. Who won? I neither know nor care. On reflection, where did those boots come from? I have no idea – I certainly had none of my own.

- The only other way my being Welsh impinged on my first year was when, at Passfield Hall, I overheard one of my fellow students talking in what I was convinced was a Welsh accent. Not only Welsh, but south Walian. And not only south Walian, but from the Rhondda, even from my parents' village of Ferndale. Though generally dark, his face was pallid (from years down the mine, I imagined), he had deep blue-black hair, and was heavily unshaven. I engaged him in conversation, and triumphantly told him my conclusions about his origins.

He laughed. He wasn't Welsh. He was Jamaican.

In my second year

Oddly, in my second year, very little that happened arose from my origins:

- My fondness for beer continued unabated. I've heard it said that the Welsh are either boozers or teetotal. I wasn't teetotal.

- In March 1966, I was told that a pub off Oxford Street was a great place to be, if you were Welsh, on St David's Day. On account of the landlord and landlady being Welsh. So I tracked it down. What a night! What happened to licensed hours? In a pub, you don't expect to see the landlady, long after closing time, standing on a table, singing 'Myfanwy' with tears in her eyes. Or the landlord looking fiercely at you and saying, 'You're a Celt'. Now this was a sore point. I'd always thought of the Celts as being the archetypal south Walian – short, dark, intense. Not like me. 'No, no,' he said. 'You're the typical Celt – fair haired, blue-eyed, and with a distant look in your eye.' I rather liked that, though I took it with a pinch of salt.

And it really was a great night.

In my final year

Towards the end of my final year I ended up in a squalid flat on Gray's Inn Road. I soon realised that the London Welsh Club stood a few hundred yards up the road towards King's Cross. Fate could not have been clearer in its intentions.

I walked into the club's impressive red-brick building. I explained my credentials. I was welcomed like a long-lost son. 'Have a look around,' the receptionist said with a lovely Welsh lilt, 'See what you think.' I set off. Then, as an afterthought, turned back to ask, 'Where's the bar?'

'Oh,' she said, 'We're not licensed.'

Bugger!

The crunch

Setting off in life has got to be stressful. Life-shaping decisions have to be made – with whom to spend it, for example, and where. When they have to be made simultaneously, you'd expect it to be traumatic. When it coincides, too, with the conclusion of a full-time education that started when you were a toddler, and the consequent urgent need for paid employment, it could almost considered cataclysmic. Yet I look back at the start of my own marriage and career with fondness.

Decision 1: Marriage

I proposed to my girlfriend in my last term at university. We were sitting in her car, an MG 1100 with a sporty Speedwell-converted engine (and no, that's not why I asked her to marry me) one evening, around the corner from the London School of Economics. All hell had been breaking loose at LSE, the student body was on strike, and we'd just been enthusiastic participants in a sit-in (it was in March 1967, if you want to look it up). We were discussing our future. I would be leaving LSE in the next few months, she still had a year to go till she completed her teaching qualification. The conversation went something like this:

Me: I could do a Postgraduate Certificate in Education, so we'd be finishing college at the same time, then we could try to find teaching jobs in the same area.

She: Mmm.

Me: I don't know how easy it would be to do that. I don't suppose education authorities would take into account that we're going out together.

She: No, I don't suppose they would.

Me: They might, if we were married.

She, looking sceptical: Are you proposing?

Me: I suppose so.

Long pause.

She: OK.

I returned to my hall of residence, she to her student digs. Both thinking, no doubt, 'Bloody hell, I'm engaged!'

If there is any more romantic account of a Welshman 'popping the question', I'd like to hear it.

So with marriage decided, it remained to sort out careers.

Decision 2: Career

Some people know, from an early age, exactly what they want to do in life. They have a dream, and they pursue it with cold logic and a single-minded determination. These are the ones, I would guess, that reach the heights in their chosen profession.

The rest of us don't have a clue. Staying in education has always been an ever-popular short-term way of putting off the evil day when you actually have to decide. At the end of college, though, that evil day arrives.

Like many people who don't know what they want to do, I decided to become a teacher. A cliché I know. But in my defence, I'm from a family of teachers. So we're obviously dedicated to the education of the young. Or terminally indecisive.

To become a teacher I needed two qualifications:

1. A degree.

A few months after I became engaged, I scraped through my university finals, getting a 'Third-Class Honours degree'. Now a third, for those unfamiliar with educational awards, is not considered to be the peak of academic achievement. Poet Philip Larkin called it 'the hallmark of imbecility'. Easy for him to say – he got a first. But I put a brave face on things. Standing on results day in front of the list posted on the noticeboard, and recovering from my astonishment that my name was included at all, I quickly totted up the numbers. I ignored the endless columns of commonplace upper and lower seconds, and concentrated on the peripheries. Six LSE students had achieved firsts, and six thirds. I was cock-a-hoop. A third was as hard to get as a first! Houghton Street was undoubtedly awash that day with sobbing upper seconds devastated by their failure to achieve firsts, hundreds more lower seconds distraught that they'd perhaps, by a whisker, missed thirds.

This argument, I would now in old age admit, didn't even persuade me, never mind anybody else. Although I'd had a great three years at LSE, I felt I'd let my parents down. Mum, bless her, sent me a letter of congratulation addressed to 'Mr J Simon, BSc (Econ)'. I don't think it was tongue-in-cheek – she was just being kind. And, fair play, it cheered me up no end. I was, after all, the first of the north Wales branch of the Simon/Hughes family to get a degree. Followed years later by my younger brother Chris, who also got a third.

I'll leave it to him to contextualise.

2.   A postgraduate teaching certificate.

A year later, at Whitelands College in south London, I scraped through my Postgraduate Certificate in Education (PGCE) exam, though again with no flying colours. On one question (about the environment) I based my entire answer on an article I'd read in *Tit-Bits*. Despite its name, this was not a pornographic, or at least not a very pornographic magazine. It's sometimes described as an early precursor of the *Daily Mail* or even the *Sun*. I'm not proud of this, but credit where credit's due.

Now that we'd assembled the necessary paperwork (my wife had duly achieved her Teacher's Certificate), it remained for us to find an education authority willing to take us on. We tried three places (Crawley, Lancaster and Ipswich). The only one to offer us work was Ipswich.

Why didn't we apply for teaching posts in Wales? Two reasons:

  o   My Welsh wasn't good enough. 'O' Level Welsh 'O2' doesn't exactly prepare you to teach your subject through the medium of Europe's oldest living language.

o My wife's Welsh was even worse than mine. In fact it was non-existent. Of course it was. She's Greek Cypriot.

Teaching jobs in Wales, then, were out of the question. So we gratefully accepted Suffolk's offer, and moved to Ipswich.

Chapter 6

A Welshman in East Anglia

WHEN MY WIFE of two months and I arrived in Suffolk in 1968 we came to it with fresh eyes. We'd never visited the area, nor had ever known, or even knowingly met, anybody from that far east. But I was pretty sure that it would turn out to be totally different from north Wales:

- It would be flat, whereas Wales was mountainous.
- Its rivers would be slow moving, whereas Welsh rivers were turbulent.
- Its buildings would be timber-framed, filled in with wattle and daub or brick, roofed with thatch or clay tiles, whereas Welsh buildings were made of stone, roofed with slate.
- Its people would be Scandinavian (tall, blond, blue-eyed and phlegmatic), not Celtic (short, dark-haired, brown-eyed and mercurial).

I really wasn't sure how we'd take to Suffolk.

We loved it.

There are few greater pleasures in life than settling in, then exploring, a part of the country you've never visited before. Especially one that is the antithesis of where you were brought up.

To start with we were pretty much restricted to Ipswich, by bus and on foot – our car's engine (yes, the Speedwell conversion) had exploded on our honeymoon drive to Greece. We had to complete the journey to Athens by train, and I returned to England in a car (a Hillman Super Minx estate) with my new wife, my mother-in-law and my eight months pregnant sister-in-law. They slept in the back, I slept across the front seats, curled around the gear lever. It took five days. But that's another story.

During our first year in Ipswich we lived in a village, Chelmondiston, five miles down the Orwell from the town.

Ipswich was just what I'd expected – a rural market town, packed with history. Which was just as well, since that's what I'd be teaching. It had a medieval street plan, lots of old houses and napped-flint-covered churches dating back to the Middle Ages or before, an old-fashioned museum. The town famously gave birth to Cardinal Wolsey, who was Henry VIII's right-hand man. Until he wasn't. It also had a recently promoted First Division football team in which I wasn't interested – that came later.

When we got our car back (with a newly reconditioned, but non-Speedwell engine) we were able to travel further afield. The more we drove around Suffolk the more we thanked the gods that had sent us there. It wasn't Wales, true – no mountains (though not quite as flat as we'd expected). No language of its own (though at times the accent made it seem as if it did). With our new motorised freedom, we ranged far and wide. Taking in its small towns. Its pretty villages. Its attractive coast. Enjoying pubs of surpassing beauty. They sold beers I'd never heard of (Tolly Cobbold, Adnams, Green King), some had peculiar pool-like tables (called, I discovered, 'bar billiards') with holes and wooden mushrooms. One pub had a game consisting of a bull's nose-ring on a cord which you had try to swing onto a beam-mounted hook. There's not much to do in rural Suffolk. All used dartboards with huge sections in multiples of five.

Not only were these dartboards easier to play on, especially when you'd had a few, but the scoring was brilliant – instead of having to count backwards and pollute your fingers with chalk dust, you simply had to move a peg on a crib-board! Just as you began to feel as if you'd gone back to the eighteenth or nineteenth century, you'd hear broad American accents, or hear the roar of heavy bombers overhead, courtesy of several nearby USAF bases.

On my first day at my first school, Copleston Boys, two things reminded me of home:

- As I was passing the school office, the secretary called out, 'Mr Simon!' I whipped around in confusion. What was Dad doing here? Then I realised. *I* was Mr Simon. Not the head of Penlleiniau school in Pwllheli, but a newly-qualified teacher in a secondary modern school in Ipswich. My son has since said that the same thing happened to him on *his* first day as a teacher, though in London not in Suffolk.

- During an early staffroom break, one of the teachers (big, bluff, with an RAF handlebar moustache) asked me where I was from. When I said 'Pwllheli', he embarked on a wartime anecdote which reflected well on Llŷn in general and its police force in particular. 'We were coming back from a bombing raid,' he said, 'badly damaged. We'd been diverted to RAF Penrhos, and were limping in across Cardigan Bay. A local bobby, seeing what was going on and with great presence of mind, stopped the traffic on both sides of the road from Pwllheli to Llanbedrog, so that we had a clear approach with no danger to civilian traffic.'

Thereafter I discovered that among grown-ups work is one of the main generators of social life, especially if you're in an area where you don't know anybody. But, surprisingly, since I was so far from Wales, it was fellow Welshmen on the staff who expanded my social circle and my range of interests. I mentioned them briefly in my first book – since both books are about my Welsh background, some overlap was inevitable:

1. Dick Hannaford, a woodwork teacher from south Wales, took me sailing on the Orwell. My experience of sailing was limited to watching yachts from Abersoch, spinnakers billowing, out on Cardigan Bay. It looked so effortlessly beautiful. Crewing on a sailing dinghy, it turned out, is – well – a different kettle of fish. Dick kept yelling incomprehensible nautical instructions at me involving sheets and dagger-boards. Our friendship survived. Just. After school, Dick helped me build a bookshelf. My grandson still uses it, fifty-five years later. Dick would have been proud! He also offered a master-class in how to deal with management hierarchies. He'd been having heated words with his head of department in the marking area, just off the staffroom. The shouting stopped, and we all waited with bated breath. Dick stormed into the main staffroom, turned back towards his red-faced HoD who was following him out, and said, 'And you can put that where the monkey puts his nuts.' I like to think that we Welsh don't respond well to intimidation.

2. Mike Evans, from Aberporth, got me involved in playing rugby for the Orwell Works of Ransome, Simms and Jeffreys, one of Ipswich's agricultural machinery manufacturers. The local football team are called the Tractor Boys for a reason. We were the two guest players allowed. I loved it. Even playing against a super-fit Borstal team on a wet Saturday afternoon, who ran rings around us physically (and yet we won), or losing to a far better team who, much to our embarrassment, also beat us at the drinking contests in the clubhouse afterwards.

It was a weekend with Mike and his wife that led to Copleston's head having to take me home in the middle of the morning. I wasn't ill, I was hungover. I still feel guilty about that.

3. Dai Williams, Head of Geography and a dyed-in-the-wool Labour party activist from the Valleys, taught me how to organise a ward during elections, something I put into practice later on in my Suffolk life.

Living in Ipswich, although we were over three hundred miles from Pwllheli, I didn't feel that far away:

- My parents came down to stay with us. Mum said she'd always hankered after a brand-new house, until she lay in bed upstairs in ours, listening to me turning over the pages of my newspaper in the lounge. 'The walls are very thin,' she observed. We went bowling in town, and Dad lost, grumbling that his thumb was swollen, and didn't fit properly into the bowling ball. But, given the distances involved, such events were infrequent. We had a phone installed, so that we could stay in touch.

- Dad and my younger brother Chris drove across country from Pwllheli to Ipswich. To surprise us. They certainly did – we were in Doncaster, staying with my older brother Jeff and his wife Ambo.

- We drove back and forth to Pwllheli – to visit family members, to go out with the boys, to attend Jonesy and Carol's wedding in Llanbedrog's tiny church. We visited Garnett and Alwena (and their new arrival Jason) just outside Chester. Yes, we were growing up.

- Though the influence of Wales wasn't quite as emphatic in my second school as in my first, there was still a notable Welsh contingent – the head was Welsh, as was one of the heads of house.

- My elevation, after a year, to Head of History, caused some comment. There were two other candidates, both external, both of whom dropped out on the morning of the interview. When I was confirmed as Head of History (yes, yes, I was the only one left standing, but I still feel I deserved it), the Welsh head of house, congratulating me, implied that the 'taffia' had seen off the other candidates. He didn't mention horses' heads, but I caught his drift.

- I met the Welsh caretaker of the special school next door, a native of Porthmadog, who was on the point of retiring after living and working and raising his kids in Ipswich for a quarter of a century. 'I'm going back to Port,' he told me. 'Why's that?' I enquired. 'I don't like it here,' he replied.

CHAPTER 7

A Welshman in North Staffordshire

In 1980 I got a job as Head of Humanities in a north Staffordshire school, and so we left Suffolk.

Though Newcastle-under-Lyme (part of the Stoke-on-Trent conurbation, though its inhabitants would indignantly deny it) was the nearest I'd lived to Wales since leaving Pwllheli, the Welsh influences were not particularly apparent:

- I noticed the odd Welsh house-name (miners, no doubt, who'd moved to the north Staffordshire coalfield for work).

- Everybody I met, it seemed, had at some point been on holiday in north Wales, and many had very strong connections, from childhood holidays or, in one case (a fellow deputy-head I taught with in Stoke), from having retired parents living in Prestatyn. Whenever he visited them, he had to take a boot-full of Staffordshire oatcakes, frozen and encased in newspaper, to feed their addiction. In those days, you couldn't get them outside the Potteries.

- My job was in a pit village, Halmerend, and I immediately discovered that the local mine (now long gone) had been the site of a major disaster. This reminded me of the south Wales pit village my parents came from – same strong local community, same memories of past deaths in the mine. I even, in my first year, ended up taking rugby practice in the shadow of the winding gear of a nearby pithead. It warmed the cockles of my little Welsh heart. It was England, but it felt Welsh.

- Visits to Pwllheli became easier – cross-country via Ruabon, Llangollen, Bala and Porthmadog.

- My father, as I said earlier a keen amateur potter, had often visited Stoke to buy equipment and clay. Unfortunately, we didn't settle there until six years after he died. He would have loved having a local contact in the area, and somewhere to stay.

- I immediately took to the Potteries. I read novels by Arnold Bennett, I visited the famous potbanks, I walked the canals, I gloried in the history of a ceramics industry that once dominated the world. I even went to watch Stoke City and Port Vale. Though not very often.

After ten years in Staffordshire we moved to Yorkshire for work.

CHAPTER 8

A Welshman in South Yorkshire

I HAVE TO admit that links between my time in Yorkshire and my homeland are not self-evident, even to me. Perhaps it was just that I no longer needed my Welsh comfort blanket. I racked my brains.

We lived in the Metropolitan Borough of Rotherham, and this gives me the only two Welsh connections – and those very tenuous – that I could think of:

- Our house was in an outlying village called Maltby – yet another of the coal-mining settlements that seem to dominate both my and my family's history.

- Another of its outlying villages was called 'Wales'. I once had to visit a school there, allowing me to surprise my wife with the statement, 'I'm off to Wales this afternoon'.

Pathetic, but that, I'm afraid, is my best shot.

I retired, my wife moved from headship into advisory and support work. We thought that that was that, that we'd end our days on the wrong side of the Pennines. Then, after twenty years, my daughter surprised us by announcing that she was moving back to Newcastle-under-Lyme with our three grandchildren ('I had such a happy childhood there,' she said. Flatterer!). So, a few months later, we followed them. That was in 2011, and we're still there.

Conclusion

So it seems emphatic. My gut feeling – that during my English exile I've drifted away from my roots – is proved beyond doubt. Being Welsh started to become an increasingly minor part of who I was, compared to my family, my friendships, my career, my political leanings, my football affiliation, my taste in food and drink and music.

Consider: I've lived in four different parts of England during the last fifty-five years of my life, and these are the average number of words I've expended on each in this part of the book:

- London – 4 years, 1,810 words (452.5 words per year).
- Suffolk – 12 years, 1,092 words (91 words per year).
- Staffordshire – 22 years, 284 words (12.9 words per year).
- Yorkshire – 20 years, 77 words (3.85 words per year).

The figures prove it – you can't argue with statistics!

And yet, and yet, this isn't *quite* true. Further digging in the garden of my memory revealed something that I really hadn't expected.

Read on!

Part Three

Keeping in Touch

One of the few benefits of old age (apart from not being dead) is having the time to think about your life. I recently moved house. In the run-up to the big day, I spent a lot of time sorting through stuff – old photographs, forgotten computer files, boxes of clippings, diaries. And I unearthed a number of ways in which, much to my surprise and with no deliberate intention at the time, I actually stayed in touch pretty effectively with Wales. They refreshed the memories, and even added to my knowledge of the country of my birth.

CHAPTER 9

Through writing

ONE OF THESE ways was through writing. Not the definitive twentieth-century Welsh novel, alas, but touring articles for caravan magazines. Now this might seem, on the travel-writing continuum, small beer, but it takes as much research to write for *Practical Caravan* as it does for Condé Nast or the *Sunday Times Travel Magazine*. Well, almost. And the great benefit for me, apart from the less than princely sums I was paid, was that, not only did it help to keep me in touch with my roots, but I even got to know areas of Wales about which I knew little or nothing. Rummaging through my clippings, I came up with three of my earliest magazine articles:

'The Forgotten Peninsula'

To start with, baby steps. When I wrote my first article on Wales, I was still working as the head of a comp. Which kept me busy. So it was a no-brainer that I should write about somewhere that needed virtually no research, somewhere I knew well. A no-brainer indeed. Llŷn. The piece, written for *Practical Caravan Magazine*, was called 'The Forgotten Peninsula'. Forgotten not by me but, I felt, by many of the hordes of visitors who flood into north Wales every summer.

This was the introduction to that first article:

To the majority of Brits, north Wales means the mountains of Snowdonia, the beaches of Rhyl and Prestatyn and Anglesey, the castles at Conway and Caernarfon and Beaumaris. But there's another north Wales, one that many people miss. It's called the Llŷn Peninsula, and it's barely three hour's drive from the big-city rush and hurry of Liverpool, Manchester and Stoke. Llŷn is a quiet, peaceful finger of land, washed by the Irish Sea, aflame with heather, gorse and rhododendron, and ringing to the sound of curlew and skylark. Its people are descended, not from Angles or Saxons, but from Brythonic Celts. Many speak little English from autumn to spring and concern themselves with the land and the sea and their own lives, cut off from the rest of the UK by a formidable mountain range. Because of its foreignness, its different language and culture – and not least its proximity – it's an ideal destination for a weekend break, or even an extended holiday, in the caravan.

It might seem a bit dewy-eyed, even for 1998 when the article was published. But I think that it still applies. I was writing for mainly English caravanners. Many parts of Britain have beautiful beaches, lovely countryside, peace and tranquillity, but none (sorry Cornwall, sorry Scotland) have their own flourishing language and culture, and none are so close to England's heartland. North Wales in general, and Llŷn in particular, are held in huge affection by people I've met in Liverpool, Manchester and the Midlands. I live in north Staffordshire, and almost everybody I know has fond childhood memories of holidays in north Wales.

The places I covered in the article were ones I knew because I was born and raised on Llŷn – Pwllheli, Llanbedrog, Criccieth, Abersoch, Nefyn, Aberdaron, Porthmadog and villages in between. I covered, too, many of the obvious tourist attractions – Butlins (OK, Hafan-y-Môr), Lloyd George's grave, the Ranch Rabbit Farm, Criccieth castle, Black Rock Sands, the Ffestiniog Railway, Porthmadog and Tremadog. All known to me, and teeming with memories from my childhood and adolescence and from visits with my kids.

Writing the piece was a doddle. I didn't have to do any research. I didn't even have to take photographs – I already had loads. All I had to do was remember.

'Great Escapes: Llŷn'

My next feature on Llŷn (for the same magazine), was six years later. I was now retired, so I had more time to put my shoulder to the wheel. Which was just as well – for 'Great Escapes: Llŷn' I had seven pages to fill, instead of the original three. I did a tour of the peninsula and filled out the original article with additional material.

The introduction was much the same (recycling's good, right?) though with this addition: 'It's the Welsh culture that makes Llŷn such an enticing Great Escape. It's like going abroad, but without the ferry charges.'

I continued with, 'Most towns and villages on Llŷn are thriving communities, though one stopped flourishing 2,000 years ago, and another died and was then resurrected.' A nice teaser that I should have left unanswered till the end, but, callow youth that I was (I was fifty-seven), answered immediately with descriptions of Tre'r Ceiri (an iron-age hill settlement) and Nant Gwrtheyrn (an abandoned quarry village revived as a Welsh-language centre). The mystery having been ruined by premature elucidation, I plodded on through Nefyn, Morfa Nefyn, Aberdaron, Pwllheli, Cricieth and Porthmadog.

I went on to: 'Llŷn has been a holiday hotspot ever since the railways arrived. In the early days it was largely adult-orientated, but increasingly the first law of family life kicked in – happy kids make happy adults.' There were plenty of fun things to do, accessible from, if not all actually on, Llŷn. Finally I offered a treasure trove of detail about what was on offer at the time: beaches, surfing, sailing, boat trips, fishing, diving, maritime museums.

During the research I learned a lot about Llŷn that I didn't know before – stuff about Abersoch's surfer-dude vibe, Hafan

Pwllheli's growing popularity, coastal boat trips and wildlife spotting, ropeworks and hovercraft rides. I enjoyed the visiting and the writing – the sidebars and contact details not so much.

This type of article – more research, fewer anecdotes, a lot of drudgery – was less fun than the simple account of a holiday, but paid better. And I did learn a lot about Llŷn that, despite being a local, I hadn't known before.

In between the two pieces about Llŷn I did a 'following in the footsteps of...' piece about George Borrow doing the research for which I absolutely loved. That's up next.

Wild Wales

In between the publication of the two articles about Llŷn, I read a book called *Wild Wales* by George Borrow. He was an East Anglian writer and eccentric who fell in love with our country and embarked on a walking tour, north to south, in the mid nineteenth century. 'Let's follow in his footsteps,' I suggested to my wife, 'at least part of the way'. We caravanners are always looking for 'missions' to excuse our wanderings.

Though Borrow started in Chester, we aimed to join him in Bala. After setting up at Pen-y-Bont campsite on Bala Lake's far shore, I went into town and the White Lion. As I sat quaffing my beer (they seemed to do a lot of quaffing back then), the late twentieth-century bar faded, and I saw it through Borrow's eyes. 'The room presented an agreeable contrast to the gloomy, desolate places through which I had lately come. A good fire blazed in the grate, and there were four tallow lights on the table.' The ghosts of the people that Borrow met a century and a half earlier crowded around me – the 'freckled maid', the 'immense man weighing 18 stone'. Alcohol doesn't half stimulate the imagination.

Next day it was off to see the spectacular waterfall Pistyll Rhaeadr. We stopped at the Wynnstay Arms. It didn't get a glowing review from Borrow: 'It seemed very large but didn't look very cheerful.' Not much change there then – it was dowdy, the landlord had never heard of George Borrow and wasn't in the least bit interested.

The waterfall hadn't changed – 'An immense skein of silk agitated and disturbed by tempestuous blasts... in winter it roars like thunder or a mad bull.' Following Borrow, we took refreshment (Victorian phrases are catching) at a small white café in front of the falls. We sat outdoors, surrounded by hundreds of chaffinches competing for crumbs. As I ordered the drinks, I asked the woman behind the counter about the visitors' book that Borrow had signed. 'It recently disappeared,' she told me. It had survived for 150 years then disappeared just before I arrived. I didn't believe a word of it.

Next day we moved on to Gigrin Farm, just outside Rhayader. Watching red kites feeding, we chatted to the farmer. 'People all over the world can watch on the internet,' he told us, 'thanks to a steerable video camera installed by the University of Wales.' A farm building had been converted into a comprehensive visitors' centre. He told us about his good relationship with Sky Television and the BBC (presumably regarding the red kite broadcasts). A beautiful white peacock cried from the roof of a nearby shed. 'He's called Persil,' the farmer said, then looked thoughtful. 'I wonder if the washing powder company would be interested in an advertising deal?' I began to appreciate why Gigrin Farm was so successful.

That evening I walked down through the village and out to a pub across the river in Cwmdeuddwr called 'The Triangle'. It was built in the sixteenth century to serve drovers herding cattle from Cardigan to London and monks travelling to the monastery of Strata Florida. I couldn't help wondering how the two lots of clientele got on.

The toilet was across the road – fine on this lovely spring evening, not so good, perhaps, in the depths of winter. The roof of the bar was so low that darts players had to open a trapdoor and stand in the space underneath to avoid spearing the ceiling. The landlord stood at one end of the bar, having a crafty smoke while keeping a weather eye open for his missus. I sat with my pint, surrounded by locals chatting and arguing. Several complained that, drawing their water from the same Elan Valley dams that supplied Birmingham, Rhayader often suffered hosepipe bans while England's second city blithely sprinkled away to their hearts content. Borrow didn't, as far as I know, stop at the Triangle Inn, but I felt that his spirit wasn't far away. And he didn't describe the Elan Valley dams either – by the time they were built, he had gone to meet his maker.

After an exhausting visit to Devil's Bridge (the path down to the river then back up again nearly killed me) we ended our Borrow trip at the Strata Florida monastery. Dafydd ap Gwilym, one of Wales's greatest poets is buried under a yew tree in the cemetery. A translation of one of his poems ('Merched Llanbadarn' – the Girls of Llanbadarn) was on show in the monastery bookshop. In it he bemoans the fact that, however hard he tries (even in church), he never gets anywhere with them. It seemed incredibly modern, considering that it was written in the thirteenth century.

Before we left we stood respectfully before a monument to a man's left leg, amputated in the eighteenth century. Talk about one foot in the grave! The rest of him emigrated to America.

The enjoyment of travel is enhanced by a good companion, and on this trip we had one of the best. Indefatigable, opinionated, well-informed if a little pompous, George Borrow gave us huge pleasure as his nineteenth-century view of mid Wales superimposed itself on our own late twentieth-century one. And having a *virtual* companion like Borrow had one great advantage. When his know-all garrulousness became unbearable, when I really couldn't stand him any more, I simply had to snap *Wild Wales* shut, and he disappeared, like a genie returning to its lamp.

I bet he was harder to shut up when he was alive!

Through writing – postscript

My two glowing caravan magazine reviews of Llŷn came in for a fair kicking – not for finding the peninsula beautiful, but for encouraging visitors to do what they do – visit.

1. Porthdinllaen in August was described as a hell-hole, with (for example) queues for beer at the Tŷ Coch snaking across the beach. This expanded into a cry of despondency about local properties being bought as holiday homes, about the flood of incomers, about the loss of Welsh identity of the area. All really serious problems for which no solutions have yet been found.

2. Faced with the accusation that my articles may have led to Llŷn being 'swamped by visitors and incomers', I could only offer the excuse that I was sure that not many people actually read them, and that even fewer were likely to have acted upon them. For those who did – both of them – I'm truly sorry. But again I accept, this is a really knotty problem with serious consequences for the whole of the peninsula.

3. A more light-hearted discussion led to a well-known Welsh aphorism which, with my imperfect Welsh, I'll try to record. It refers to the breaking of wind:
   '*Cyntaf clyw, hynny yw*' (the first to smell it is the one who did it). Which often, in my memory, led to the response, '*Yr ail a gegodd, hynny rhechodd*' (the second to speak of it is the one who did it'). The person who brought this up (I will mention no names – OK Pauline) can be relied upon to lower the tone.

4. I agreed that the word '*Sglyfath*' is an excellent word, useful in all sorts of contexts. Though the only word I could find that's anything like it in the dictionary was '*ysglyfaeth*' which means 'prey' or 'victim'. This didn't really chime with my understanding of '*sglyfath*' as being 'you dirty bugger.' There was much discussion, and

general agreement that my understanding of the word was correct.

As for *Wild Wales*, a number of points were made:

- I'll kick off with a comment that pleased me no end – in my writing, I was told, I'm less pompous than George Borrow. Faint praise, perhaps, but take your encouragement where you find it.

- A member of the group used to dine at the Wynnstay Arms when visiting her brother at his Oswestry private school. This in turn led to a comment from a friend of hers who'd noticed that he'd disappeared from Ysgol Ramedeg Pwllheli, and had wondered where he'd gone. That seemed to happen a lot in Llŷn – kids you knew suddently disappeared, swallowed up by the private sector, never to be heard of again.

- Another member of the group posted a YouTube link to a *Wild Wales* reading, which was excellent. All hail Facebook.

- 'Strata Florida' it was thought sounded like a pretentious name for a holiday home. Compared to the Welsh version – 'Ystrad Fflur' – which sounds beautiful. Prompting further approbation of the movement to start calling Welsh towns, places, mountains and everything else by their Welsh, not their English names. Sometimes to us Anglophone Welsh folk it feels odd, but really well worth the effort.

Chirk

I've also got George Borrow to thank for getting me to write about Chirk, though I'd been to the town many years before. When I was a teenager, a group of us from Pwllheli joined a trip to Llangollen, nominally to go to the Eisteddfod, but in fact to say that we'd had a pint on Sunday. At that time, like many other parts of Wales, Dwyfor (the area around Pwllheli) was dry on the Sabbath. Indeed, Dwyfor was to stay dry, off and on, until 1996 – the last bastion of Sunday closing in Wales. From Llangollen we caught a bus to Chirk, then walked down to the Bridge Inn for a pint, just over the border in England. My only comment now, in old age, would be, 'Were we stark raving mad?' Bearing in mind that travel sickness was (and still is) the bane of my life, I signed up for a bus trip, on narrow winding Welsh roads, of around 140 miles in total, just to say that I'd had a pint on a Sunday. Even though it involved several pints, and turned out to be a really good session, it still seems insane. In my defence, I was sixteen, and that's an age not known for common sense.

But to get back to the later visit, about which I wrote in *Practical Motorhome*. Although it was *Wild Wales* that prompted me to later revisit Chirk, the final piece owed nothing to George Borrow's description. He confined himself to Chirk Castle, and there was little correspondence between his description of what it looked like in the mid nineteenth century and what it looked like at the start of the twenty-first. But there was a lot else, in the castle and in the town, that was worth writing about:

- The castle was pristine, with elegant grounds. Inside, a compilation of the owner's family home-movies led me to have real sympathy for him, not something I normally feel for nobs who own castles. He was saying how useless he felt in comparison with the people who worked for him – people with useful, hard-earned and admirable skills, things which he felt that he couldn't claim to possess. Full marks to him for not only recognising it, but for admitting it in public. Shades of Lord Ralph and his relationship with his Irish estate worker Ted on the *Fast Show*.

- Telford's majestic aqueduct, carrying the Llangollen Canal over the valley, was (and presumably still is) hugely impressive, shadowed by the later railway viaduct right next to it. Lucky residents can walk their dogs along the aqueduct towpath, high above the river and with spectacular views, then go through the long canal tunnel (in my case using the torch on my phone), emerging on the road to the railway station.

- St Mary's Church made me smile at the monument to a Crusader, killed in the Holy Land. They couldn't bring his whole body back, so settled for just his heart. As I entered the church the organ was being tuned. That is, the church organ, not the crusader's heart! Having, as a child, often helped the organ tuner in St Peter's in Pwllheli, I was able to swap anecdotes with the guy who was sitting at the keyboard while his mate clambered about among the pipes.

- The Hand Hotel, built in 1610, is one of the oldest hotels in Wales, and was very atmospheric, very pleasant. The bar was thronged with locals, whose conversation gave me a good introduction to the area. Since getting older and totally shameless, I have no qualms about eavesdropping. They talked mainly of farming and the approach of Christmas.

- The highlight of my visit was to the Bridge Inn. I didn't expect the landlord to remember me – two visits, forty years apart, hardly made me a regular. He might even have been the original landlord's son. As I ordered my pint in the long public bar, I asked if we were in England or Wales. He said, 'Here we're in England but ...' nodding to the group of old men at the other end of the bar, '... there they're in Wales.' 'I better move then,' I said, and carried my pint along to join them. There followed a convivial evening, in a mixture of English and Welsh, with several rounds and a choice of free cheeses from a plate on the bar.

CHAPTER 10

Through caravanning

I'VE HAD OTHER visits to Wales that haven't been as easy to summon up because I never got round to writing about them, so I've got no clippings to consult. Notebooks perhaps, but they're very patchy.

South-west Wales

A tour of south-west Wales included St Davids, Tenby and Laugharne. I was initially underwhelmed by St Davids Cathedral, but I've since been mightily impressed by photographs and videos I've seen of it.

The Pembrokeshire coast was rugged, and included a seal-spotting trip on an inshore inflatable. We saw only one seal, however, some distance away in a small cove. I wondered if it was an inflatable, put on the beach to stop disappointed customers demanding refunds.

Tenby was as beautiful as it looks on all the travel programmes.

In Laugharne I got my wife to take a picture of me standing outside Dylan Thomas's boathouse – it would come in handy when I became a celebrated poet. Never mind that I don't write poetry. In Laugharne itself we went for a drink in Brown's Hotel, where we were steamrollered into conversation by a good-natured but very drunk and insistent man. I'd have complained, but he was really big. And it was in keeping with our reason for being there – it was Dylan Thomas's favourite pub. I even wondered if our tipsy tormentor was employed by the tourist board to add colour, and wasn't drunk at all. It was, after all, only eleven o'clock in the morning.

Hay-on-Wye

We visited the Hay-on-Wye book festival twice, seeing a host of world-renowned writers going through their paces on stage in the main tent. But nothing stayed in my mind except for the endless earnest questions put from the floor by people who were seeking to show off their erudition rather than searching for enlightenment. It's odd. I don't remember any of the speakers or anything that they said. But I clearly remember seeing Martin Amis in town. He was with his wife, and he was pushing a pram. He was shorter than I expected.

Cardiff

I'd visited our capital often in the murky mists of the past – on school trips to watch rugby internationals, when visiting family in the Rhondda, even on a camping trip after I got married. All this was before I started writing travel articles, so I have no written accounts to jog my memory. On that last camping weekend we had fish and chips in Harry Ramsden's, famous for its chandeliers and for visits by the Welsh National Opera company. The chandeliers were there, but not the Welsh National Opera. And that's all I remember.

Much more recently (like last year), we spent our final days as caravanners in Cardiff. No, we're not divorced, and neither of us has died. We'd decided to sell the campervan and buy a static in north Wales. The campsite was right in the centre of the city, an easy parkland walk from the castle. And though we were only stopping for a couple of days, those days were packed with highlights:

- On our first stroll through the city centre we passed a

busker. OK, big deal. But she was playing a harp. Classy or what?

- We caught a bus down to Cardiff Bay. We couldn't take a boat trip out to see the barrage (it was winter, and all the ferry ticket kiosks were shut), but we had an extended stroll – the Pierhead building, the Senedd, the Wales Millennium Centre, and the Norwegian Church, together with several impressive pieces of public sculpture. We ate (and drank a bottle of wine) in a Mermaid Quay restaurant, then (fuzzily) caught the bus back into the city centre. A great day out.

- A visit to the National Museum of Wales started inauspiciously. We planned to look at the museum's collection of Impressionists. 'Bad luck,' the member of staff said when we asked, 'that gallery closed yesterday for rehanging'. Was there just the hint of an amused malicious sparkle in his eye? Surely not. Serendipity came to the rescue – there was a first-rate exhibition of the photos of a well-known photographer – David Hurn. There was, too, a collection of ceramics. Despite living in the Potteries, and having tried my best, I've never been able to give ceramics the attention they no doubt deserve. There are only so many cups and saucers and teapots and milk jugs and plates you can feign an interest in, however beautiful they might be.

- As far as I was concerned, the highlight of our visit to Cardiff was Llandaff Cathedral. As the sun set we walked from the campsite to the cathedral across Pontcanna Fields, and having taken some time searching for the cathedral entrance, walked into an epiphany. The soaring architecture of the nave, the warm glow of the setting sun illuminating the stained-glass windows, the figure of Christ – Jacob Epstein's *Majestas* – soaring high above us, and the angelic voices of the girls' choir being rehearsed by a blue-cassocked choirmaster, made the whole experience an enchantment. It was almost enough to make me believe in God. On our walk back to the campsite, shadowy figures walked dogs with brightly lit collars – a new canine fashion, apparently. Crossing a park under a darkening sky with multicoloured circles of light streaking and curving and twisting hither and yon, made for a truly surreal ending to an inspiring evening. And completely free of alcohol or psychedelic drugs.

Cardiff is a capital city to be proud of. And we'd only seen a tiny portion of it. I know there are those who favour Machynlleth (a nightmare to pronounce if you're not Welsh) or Swansea (with its special place in Welsh hearts, what with Dylan Thomas and Catherine Zeta-Jones).

But hey. Cardiff *feels* like a national capital. So we should be happy with that.

Cardiff – postscript

I expected some negative comments about my positive view of Cardiff. They weren't forthcoming.

1. A fervent Swansea Jack grudgingly allowed that, when passing through Cardiff, 'it looked OK'.

2. Another visitor from north Wales loved it, even though it was on a day when Wales lost a rugby international in the city.

3. A comment that the campsite in the centre of Cardiff was 'a little gem' I took to mean a sparkling jewel, rather than a small lettuce.

Swansea

A visit to Swansea was more problematic than I'd hoped. Following advice from friends, we booked on the Heart of Wales line from Craven Arms to Swansea – they said the scenery was superb. In the event, we were told after boarding the train that a shortage of drivers meant that we'd have to get off at Llandrindod Wells and complete the journey by bus. Nearly seventy miles on narrow bendy Welsh roads, and I'm a very poor traveller if I'm not driving. By the time we got to Swansea I was an interesting shade of green. Not the first time I'd been green in Swansea – I used to pick my son up from the university, and this always involved a heavy night in the bar.

I was glad to get to the hotel for a lie down. Too easy. I'd made a mistake, and booked, not the wrong day, but the wrong month. And the hotel refused to give me a refund for the day we wouldn't be using. So I had to shell out again. The whole trip was saved only by next day's visit to the Dylan Thomas Centre, where an excellent and imaginative display about his life and work was worth the suffering.

Harlech

Our visit to Harlech was not a great success. We camped at the Caravan Club site between the castle and the sea, and it rained for the whole weekend. And I'm not talking romantic, misty Celtic drizzle, but full-on, gutter-gurgling, instant-soaking downpours. It eased up only once, and during that brief interlude we scuttled along the road to the beach. Which was, I have to say, magnificent – a huge crescent of sand with white rollers tumbling in from Cardigan Bay. But as for the rest of the weekend, we stayed in the van.

As I walked under my umbrella to the toilet block, I caught a glimpse, through the gloom and mist, of rugby posts. The playing fields of Ysgol Ardudwy. Two thoughts struck me:

- It was against Ysgol Ardudwy that I played my inaugural game of rugby in YRP's first XV. You don't forget a thing like that. I even remember the score – we won 12–3.

- A second thought quickly followed. *His Dark Materials* author Philip Pullman, six weeks my junior, spent his teenage years at Ysgol Ardudwy. So if he played rugby, and if he was in Ysgol Ardudwy's first team, it is almost certain that I played against him on that day. At last, a claim to fame worthy of the name! I've made no effort since to find out if Philip Pullman did in fact play rugby – I'd rather not know. Until proved differently, I played rugby against Philip Pullman. And won! I later came across an interview with the great man where he described an evening sitting on a window seat in his bedroom, listening to jazz, looking across Cardigan Bay towards Llŷn, and imagining that the 'little lights of Pwllheli and Cricieth twinkling in the distance' were the lights of San Francisco. No disrespect to Pwllheli and Cricieth, but that does seem a bit of a stretch. On the other hand, Pullman *is* famous for his imagination.

In the opposite direction, you can see Harlech Castle from Pwllheli. It looks really small.

Aberaeron

Aberaeron was very pretty, with multi-coloured houses that reminded me of Ireland. We had a meal at the Harbourmaster Hotel, during which we chatted with a couple at the next table. Loudly – they were the required two meters away, and we weren't at a Downing Street party.

I'm afraid that's it.

CHAPTER 11

Through sport

THERE ARE ONLY two sports that I've got any time for: rugby and football. Each, in its own way, helped me to stay connected to Wales.

Rugby

Apart from playing rugby at school, a single match at university (see above) and for a short time in Suffolk after I started teaching (again, see above), I've never been a close follower of the game. In Pwllheli, as in the rest of north Wales, football was the principal obsession – rugby was the preserve of the south. Only a handful of schools in Caernarfonshire played rugby – YRP in Pwllheli, the grammar school and Segontium Secondary Modern in Caernarfon, Friars School in Bangor and John Brights in Llandudno. This explains how I got into the county under-15s team – I was the best scrum-half of five. The school's first XV also watched internationals – on TV (often at our coach Harry Hughes's bungalow next to the school) and, once a year, live, at the Arms Park in Cardiff. But all the great Welsh clubs and players were in south Wales – the only north Walian international I can remember was Dewi Bebb, who was from Bangor. Looking back, it's no wonder that I was a Bebb fan. He was born in Bangor (like my little brother Chris), attended Friars School (against whom I'd played many times), and became a teacher via Trinity College, Carmarthen (like

155

both my father and my older brother Jeff). But despite his long and distinguished career – 221 appearances for Swansea (his only club), thirty-four Welsh caps and eight appearances for the Lions, he doesn't seem to have received the recognition he deserved.

The 1970s

However, I began to really appreciate the delights of international rugby union in the 1970s because the Welsh national team was going through an extraordinary golden age. Between 1969 and 1979, Wales won or shared eight Five Nations Championships (including three Grand Slams) and six Triple Crowns. To quote Wikipedia:

> The zenith of Welsh rugby was the 1970s, when Wales had players such as Barry John, Gareth Edwards, Phil Bennett and J P R Williams. Wales won four consecutive Triple Crowns. The strong Pontypool front row of Graham Price, Bobby Windsor and Charlie Faulkner were all manual workers, and Robin McBryde was formerly the holder of the title of Wales's strongest man. Gareth Edwards was voted the greatest player of all time in a players' poll in 2003 and scored what is widely regarded as the greatest try of all time in 1973 for the Barbarians against New Zealand.

My hero-worship of the Welsh national team wasn't only because I was Welsh, or because I played rugby myself. One clue lies in the above Wikipedia quote: 'The strong Pontypool front row... were all manual workers.' It seemed to me that, among the home nations, the Welsh team was the only one that was largely made up of ordinary working men, rather than the expensively educated middle-class public-school boys that seemed to dominate those of the other home nations. Or rather, specifically, of England. And that Welsh team (unbiased opinion) played rugby that was close to perfection.

I have to admit to being an armchair fan, a telly rather than terrace supporter. I also remained totally ignorant of all the ins and outs of club rugby, in Wales and elsewhere. So it's undoubtedly true that my fandom was skin-deep. An Arms Park patriot, if you like. But God, what a pleasure it was in the 1970s to see the scarlet hordes streaming towards opponents' try lines, and Wales bestriding Five Nations rugby like a Celtic colossus!

1980s

My experience of rugby in the 1980s, I'm ashamed to say, had everything to do with what the Irish call 'the craic' and little to do with the sport of rugby union itself. It went like this. I got a call from my older brother Jeff, who lived in Birmingham, to say that he and two (Welsh) friends were thinking of starting to go to some of Wales's away games, and would I fancy joining them? I needed time to think. All of a nano-second. That offer led directly to only three trips abroad – one to Dublin, two to Paris. And on only one of those did I actually attend a match. The other two I watched on TV, something which I could easily have done at home. I don't remember anything about the games, what the score was or even who won. As I said, it was all about the craic, not the rugby.

- The first match was against Ireland in Dublin. We met at Birmingham Airport, flew to the republic's capital and headed for Temple Bar. It's billed as the city's cultural quarter, and is packed with galleries and venues devoted to photography, the arts, drama. None of which we visited. But also pubs. All I saw of Temple Bar was the inside of one of them. We found a comfortable and very Irish alehouse. The whole time we were there a production-line of half-poured pints of Guinness shuffled along the bar, waiting their turn to be topped up and handed over. We'd bagged a corner with a good view of the telly and settled down to draw lots. I forgot to mention that we'd only managed to buy one ticket between us. And to our everlasting shame, I think that the three of us who drew the longest straws were relieved that we'd be staying in the warm and the dry, while the winner of the golden ticket left, his shoulders slumped in defeat, his face resigned, clutching his short straw. We had a great afternoon – the craic was excellent, and we were joined by a mini-bus full of ebullient south Walians who'd crossed from Swansea to Cork.

- The second match was in the Parc des Princes in Paris. This time we were better organised – we had a ticket each, and devolved responsibilities. Mine was to research, choose and book a hotel. The one I picked, as close as possible to the station, was well received by the others. It felt odd for me, a young shaver in my forties, to be asked by the patronne to keep my more elderly companions quiet when, a little the worst for wear, we got in that night.

- The trip to the third match was nearly aborted. Jeff phoned to say that the other two couldn't make it, so it was all off and he'd sell what he'd booked so far – coach tickets plus hotel. Luckily, he hadn't paid for match tickets yet. On the spur of the moment I said that I'd take two of the coach/hotel packages off his hands. Then asked my sixteen-year-old son if he fancied a weekend in Paris. He did.

  o The luxury coach journey was uneventful. I didn't even throw up. We arrived in Paris at about 5am. We were let off the coach in Montmartre for breakfast, then continued to the hotel way out in the suburbs. Having had no sleep, and without tickets to the match, I really couldn't face the hassle of attending. I decided to have a long nap and watch it on TV. My son, sixteen years old and made of sterner stuff, asked if it was OK for him to go into Paris on his own. With some misgivings I agreed. We arranged to meet on the Pont Neuf at 6pm.

o I had my sleep, I watched the match, then cadged a lift on the coach which was taking the rest of the group into the city. I was at the rendezvous at ten to six. By 6.30pm I was beginning to rough out my side of a phone conversation with my wife. Telling her that, having come to Paris with our first-born, I'd lost him. It was a conversation that I wasn't looking forward to. Then he turned up, a little surprised, I imagine, by the enthusiasm with which he was greeted.

o We had a splendid night out. We ate at McDonalds (in the capital of haute cuisine? Shame!). But it was such a thrill to get a beer in a McDonalds. Afterwards we went into a bar, ordered drinks and couldn't believe the prices. So we left, bought a load of cans in a French mini-market, then caught the Metro. We chatted to a black guy, who confirmed, over one of our cans and a political chat, that racism was a problem in France. From the station we walked back to our hotel, bought a single extortionate round of drinks at the bar, just to get the glasses, which we then surreptitiously recharged from our carrier-bag of cans. I remember nothing of the trip home, though a photograph confirms that I took a picture of my son with the Eiffel Tower in the background.

Football

I won't dwell on the football. As a child I had my heroes – the Allchurch brothers, the Charles brothers in general, and John in particular – but I wasn't really aware of international football. Dad would take me to Ninian Park when we were in south Wales, but all I remember is tea that was so foul that, at half-time, people bought a mug to warm their hands, then threw the contents away. I had a brief burst of engagement with football when Terry Yorath was manager but, when his contract wasn't renewed, felt that he'd been shabbily treated and lost interest. This interest was revived briefly under Gary Speed and continued, after his tragic death, under Chris Coleman. I admit I'm a fair weather supporter, but I consider myself fortunate that the defeat of favourites Belgium during the 2016 Euros, one of the greatest nights in Welsh football history, happened during one of my windows of enthusiasm. What a game! Belgium scored first, with a terrific goal, and it seemed that a drubbing was inevitable. When Williams equalised, it seemed like a dream, but there was a long way to go. Then Robson-Kanu put Wales into the lead with that brilliant Cruyff turn, and Vokes sealed the win with a looping header. OK, defeat to Portugal in the semi-final seemed, and turned out to be, unavoidable, but Wales had reached the semi-final in a world-class tournament, and the win over Belgium was an absolute classic.

Yes, the 2022 World Cup was hugely disappointing but, despite that, the future of Welsh football seems, at the time of writing, bright.

CHAPTER 12

Through friends

DURING MY MORE than half-century living in England, most of my friends have, not surprisingly, been English. Therefore, again unsurprisingly, they've played little part in maintaining my links with Wales. Indeed, my being Welsh only comes up at all when Wales are doing much better or much worse than are England in either rugby or football.

Even so, friends have now and again boosted my connection with my homeland.

On bikes: Brian and Phil

I met Brian and Phil when we taught at Sir Thomas Boughey High School just outside Newcastle-under-Lyme. We used to play snooker every Friday night at the 'Forty-five Club' in town.

Our cycling adventures started as an alcohol-fuelled conversation during one of these evenings. 'Let's cycle to Market Drayton!' one of us said. Almost certainly not me. But it seemed like a good idea. We discussed it enthusiastically and, from then on, frequently, but failed to put our money where our mouths were. So much so that, increasingly, each time we raised the matter, it was greeted with hoots of derision from the rest of our snooker chums and, indeed, from the whole of the club. The abuse became so intense that eventually we had to do something about it. Walk the walk (or cycle the cycle) rather than just talking the talk.

The chosen day broke dull but dry. We met (I can't remember where) and set off. It was hardly pleasant pedalling – it's main road all the way – but we arrived in Market Drayton in good order. Google Maps tells me that it's fourteen miles and takes an hour and seventeen minutes on a bike. I think it took us longer – the other two were keen cyclists, but I wasn't. I'd only bought a bike to fit in. At one point on the ride we were at loggerheads. Or, rather, at Loggerheads. It's a village on the A53.

When we got to Market Drayton, it was, aptly, market day. This was memorable for two reasons:

- I bought a small pocket edition of *Moby Dick* off a market stall. This was in the 1980s. It's now 2024. I'm about half-way through.

- The pubs had extended opening hours. All of them. We checked.

It took us a lot longer to get home. Phil got fed up and sped off ahead. Brian and I stopped at several pubs – Brian because he is, in addition to being super fit, also kind and didn't want to leave me behind; me because I was knackered, and needed to pee. I don't recommend drinking while cycling – it does little for your sense of balance. Also, stopping at pubs, though reducing the need to pee in the short-term, increases it in the long-term. But I got home in one piece. And at least, on subsequent Friday nights, nobody could take the mickey – we'd done what we set out to do. Honour was satisfied.

So far, though, no mention of Wales.

Flushed with the success of our first foray, our next was to Leek. And no, that's not the Welsh connection. Thirteen miles and an hour and twenty minutes (again according to Google Maps), it was a harder ride – you've got to cross the sprawling city of Stoke-on-Trent, and it's hillier.

Edited highlights:

- I was wearing a hat with side flaps but had failed to secure them under my chin. As I was freewheeling down a hill towards the A500 (with, I'll admit, a fair degree of *hwyl*), a car overtook me, and I saw a gaggle of kids crammed onto the back seat, pointing at me through the rear window, convulsed with laughter. Yes, the flaps were doing what flaps do (flapping). I must have looked as if I were trying to take off.

- When we got to Leek, Brian and I settled into a pub to wait for Phil. He finally staggered in, late and, unusually for him, dishevelled. Coming down the long hill into the town, with a fair degree of *hwyl* himself for an Englishman, a car had pulled out from a side road and sent him cartwheeling across its bonnet. The driver was an attractive young woman and was very penitent, so he let it go.

Apart from the town having the same name as the Welsh national vegetable, still no connection with Wales.

So, to cut to the chase. For our third adventure we decided to up the ante and go for international travel. Llangollen. Forty-eight miles, and over four hours each way. This was serious stuff – a two-day ride with an overnight stay in the land of my fathers. For six weeks beforehand I actually got up early and jogged – sometimes with my young daughter to keep me company. I really didn't want to be shamed by being left behind.

We chose our route. We selected a B&B in Llangollen which could provide secure storage for our bikes. We were waved off by our wives, who seemed distracted. Fighting back the tears, I suppose. Though sometimes their suppressed sobs sounded suspiciously like laughter.

After all this time my memories of the ride are pretty sketchy: a stop at the Hanmer Arms, Brian disappearing to fix a slow puncture, Phil forging ahead, his bobble hat floating above a distant hedge. I took lots of photos – action shots of the other two, shots of each of us against various landmarks, sitting proudly astride our bikes.

On arrival in Llangollen, we dumped our stuff at the B&B, locked our bikes in the shed, and set off for a night on the town. And this is where 'Wales' comes in. I felt so relaxed, so at home. I knew Llangollen from the many times I'd passed through on my way to Pwllheli – the turbulent river, the pretty bridge from which in summer daredevil youths jump into the Dee, the second-hand bookshop in a disused cinema, the good variety of pubs. And it's so – well – Welsh!

I have not a single memory of our return trip to Newcastle. Not because anything traumatic happened, I'm sure. I like to think it was because I was beginning to get into the groove, becoming a proper cyclist. Or perhaps the hangover had something to do with it.

Back home I opened my camera to retrieve the film.

Disaster! The camera was empty.

How to explain to Brian and Phil that I'd forgotten to load the camera with film? I thought of emigrating, but my wife wouldn't hear of it. Suicide perhaps? A bit extreme. So I had to man up and confess. I'd like to say that they took it with a rueful shake of the head and a sympathetic arm over the shoulder. But I can't. They hooted. They roared. They rushed off to tell everybody else in the club. I'll never be allowed to forget it. Ever!

The Offa's Dyke ride

Despite all my efforts to keep up, I finally had to admit that, bike-wise, I wasn't in the same league as Brian and Phil, and my only course was to bow out gracefully. However, their next epic ride – along the Welsh border with England from south to north – did confer on me two great Welsh memories, for which I thank them:

1. They were starting from Chepstow, and I agreed to meet them there to send them off in style. So they booked three rooms in a hotel, and I drove down from Pwllheli, where I was visiting my mother, to join them. Now I

had travelled from Pwllheli to south Wales many times as a child but, a martyr to car sickness, I was never in any condition to enjoy the scenery. This time, driving my own car, and alone, I could actually look around. I set off early, there was very little traffic on the road, and I finally started to understand why Wales is famous for its scenery. It was, from start to finish, so beautiful. Sunlit mountains, valleys, rivers, woodland, villages and towns flowed past the windows of my car. I arrived in Chepstow elated. My God – my home country was stunning! Our rooms in the hotel had a small common lounge, so we had a few pints, I played my guitar, and we had a singsong.

2. The second fruit of their Offa's Dyke trip didn't become apparent until much later. Among the stories of their adventures, one really stuck with me. They'd stopped at a pub in Old Radnor. The bar was full – a mixture of locals and gentle English hippies – and they looked forward to a cracking session. They'd cycled many miles, and felt they'd earned their rest and their beer. Suddenly the bar emptied, leaving only themselves and the landlord. 'Where has everybody gone?' Brian asked. 'To watch the sunset,' the landlord replied, suppressing a grin. So they left the pub, and, sure enough, in front of it stood the crowd. They were totally silent, some in a happy place of their own, some arm in arm, bathed in the fiery red and gold light in the sky above the rest of Wales to the west. When the sun finally dipped below the horizon, everybody returned to the bar and carried on drinking.

So impressed were we with this picture of a lovely pub in a lovely area, with a spiritual clientele, that nothing would do but that the rest of us Friday night snooker players (and our wives) should visit it. We arranged an overnight stay, booked bed and breakfast and an evening meal, and converged on the

Harp in Old Radnor. It was all that Brian and Phil had claimed, and we enjoyed a great evening, though without a sunset – it was overcast.

After closing time, as we sat in the residents' lounge with brandies and coffees, the landlady strode in with loaded arms and dropped onto the table packets of bacon and sausages and mushrooms and tomatoes and boxes of eggs.

'It's for your breakfast,' she said by way of explanation, and turned on her heel.

'Aren't you going to make our breakfast?' someone called out.

'Not bloody likely,' she answered. 'I'm not getting up at that time of the morning! You're welcome to use the kitchen.'

And with that she swept out of the room.

There was a stunned silence, followed by guffaws of disbelieving laughter.

And next morning that's what we did – we cooked our own breakfast.

John O'Groats to Land's End

Brian and Phil went on to greater things. Their epic ride along Offa's Dyke led eventually to a triumphant John O'Groats to Land's End marathon, the ultimate test. I offered to support them – motorhome proffers of rest, hot drinks, food, that sort of thing – but they turned me down, seeing it as a pathetic attempt to enjoy a little of their reflected glory. If only they'd taken me with them, they'd now have a photographic record of the whole trip. Or not.

On Foot: Bill and Murph

I met Bill Parkinson when I signed up for one of his adult education English Literature evening classes at Keele University. We became friends and started meeting up, accompanied by our wives, once a week, usually at the Bear on

West Brampton or the Castle Mona on Leech Street. They were keen on walking and cycling, and had done both in many parts of Wales, including the Llŷn Peninsula. They had been very taken with Llŷn, mentioning, in particular, the hymn singing wafting out of Salem chapel in Pwllheli as they came down Salem Terrace into the town.

During one of our pub sessions, Bill asked if I might be up for a walk to Llangollen. I thought he was joking, but he wasn't. Full of *hwylcwrw* (and if there isn't such a word in Welsh, there ought to be), I agreed.

Over the succeeding weeks, Bill pored over his maps, plotted a route which consisted of as little road-walking as possible, and booked accommodation. No, of course we weren't going to do it in a day – it's nearly fifty miles! There was going to be three legs – Newcastle to Wrenbury, Wrenbury to Overton, and Overton to Llangollen. My wife would pick us up in the car from Llangollen and bring us home.

I can't swear to the details of the walk – it was a long time ago. But I did take a camera, and this time remembered to load it with film.

- Early on we had to cross a field containing a bull. We could see the farmhouse with the farmer standing outside. 'Is it safe to cross the field?' Bill called out. The farmer bent his head, thought for a few seconds, and said, 'Probably.' Not very reassuring, but there was no alternative route. An enraged bull, a hectic chase, escape by a hair's breadth would have made an excellent story, but alas the bull totally ignored us. So much so that I had time to stop and take a picture of a hefty pile of bovine dung. It's not often you get the chance to capture an image of actual bullshit.

- At one point our passage along a short valley was blocked by a tall wrought-iron ornamental screen. Bill, in true leader style, clambered up it. When he sat astride the top, some thirty feet in the air, I opened the small gate that

167

I'd noticed at the base of the screen and walked through. Murph was amused. Bill wasn't.

- As we crossed the border from England into Wales, I sang '*Calon Lân*'. It should by rights have been '*Hen Wlad fy Nhadau*', but I didn't know all the words.

- We finally passed under the Pont Cysyllte aqueduct and sat down in Llangollen to wait for my wife. She brought food, we had a picnic by the river, then drove back to Newcastle.

You appreciate your homeland even more, I think, it you've worked really hard to get there.

CHAPTER 13

Through family

With brother and daughter in south Wales

My brother Jeff's son Siôn bought a house in Ferndale, the pit village in which my mother, father and uncles and aunts were born and raised. He invited his dad and me to stay, so that we could look around their old haunts. My grown-up daughter Catherine also came along. As it happened, her then-husband played bass-guitar in a band. They were recording in Rockfield Studios near Monmouth. Since it was more or less on our way, we called in. Her not-yet-ex showed us round. Our tour ended with the visitors' book.

Established on their farm by two brothers in 1960, in 1965 Rockfield became the first residential recording studio in the world. Recent research tells me that the studios have hosted a huge range of Britain's rock music elite:

1970s: Queen; Black Sabbath; Mike Oldfield; Del Shannon; Motorhead.

1980s: Simple Minds; Adam and the Ants; Clannad; The Waterboys; Robert Plant; Bauhaus; T'Pau; Fields of the Nephilim.

1990s: Stone Roses; The Pogues; Annie Lennox; Paul Weller; Oasis; Julian Lennon; Coldplay.

Also, as is seemly, a number of Welsh bands: Amen Corner;

Super Furry Animals; Manic Street Preachers; Catatonia.

Remember, this list includes only bands that I knew – there were loads of others that I'd never heard of. I don't suppose that never having been heard of by me will have done their careers any lasting harm.

It's pointless to regret the past. I certainly don't regret visiting Rockfield Studios. But I do regret that I was so uninterested in popular music from 1968 onwards that the only name that I'd recognised, under my own steam, as it were, from the galaxy of stars who will have signed the visitors' book, was Del Shannon. All the rest were introduced to me by my children, or by my own half-hearted attempts to get down with the kids. I did no research into Rockfield Studios before my visit (though in my defence, research was harder in those pre-internet days), and I was dismissive of the value of rock and pop. From the late 1960s, when I was a teacher, married and a house owner, I considered popular music to be one of the childish things the Bible told us to put away. What an idiot!

With older brother Jeff in Llantwit Major

Jeff and I visited our cousin Christine and her husband Keith in Llantwit Major. My only memory – as we negotiated the town, Jeff said, 'If this is Llantwit Major, what must Llantwit Minor be like?' I laughed. I've since researched Llantwit Major – it's twice the size of Pwllheli! That put me in my place.

With younger brother Chris in Llantwit Major

Arranged with cousin Chris (tine) and her husband Keith by my brother Chris (topher), we drove across the Severn Bridge in a howling gale. Spent the next day in Ferndale, hunting out the monuments of our grandparents (who shared a grave), our uncle Huwie (who shared the grave with his parents) and our

Auntie Kate. We walked up through Stradey Park to 2 Llŷn Crescent where our grandparents had lived and our mother and her siblings had grown up. In the park (where one of our uncles was once the park-keeper), a teacher was taking a class of small boys in the skills of rugby. They were all smart in red jerseys and were so small that the ball looked huge in their hands.

The house, and the lane behind it where sheep rummaging through the dustbins used to wake me up, looked just the same.

With the family on our daughter's fortieth birthday celebration

We stayed in yurts in Y Ffôr, showed the grandchildren around Pwllheli, and had an evening meal out. My daughter and I both had suspected food poisoning. I say 'suspected', and I won't name where we ate, because I don't want to be sued. But we were the only two who had opted for a certain seafood, and we were the only two to be ill. Needless to say, neither of us has eaten that seafood since. And being in yurts, in a field a long way from the toilets, was a bit of a downer, though when you're being sick into a river, at least the vomit is carried merrily away, and doesn't hang about in toilet bowls, making you feel even worse. Or is that over-sharing?

With my wife in Aberystwyth

When Covid restrictions were lifted, we said, 'Let's have a weekend away in Aberystwyth'. As you do. We stayed in a pub within walking distance of the town centre, listened to a folk group playing on the front, struggled to find somewhere to park. We were amazed that something as striking as the war memorial never seems to feature in photographs of the town. We took a trip on the Vale of Rheidol narrow-gauge railway to

Devil's Bridge, all masked and socially distanced. That's us, not Devil's Bridge.

I really liked Aberystwyth, and pondered that, if I'd accepted the offer of a place at Aber rather than LSE, my life would have been totally different. More involved with Wales, less with Cyprus. Wales's loss was Cyprus's gain. Or so it seems to me.

A lovely visit, but it didn't end well. My wife and I both suffered a mild dose of food poisoning. Seafood again.

With family on our golden wedding anniversary in Portmeirion

For this the family (us, our children and grandchildren, together with my brother Chris) stayed for four days in Portmeirion – we had a whole house to ourselves! The adults enjoyed exploring the village, the two youngest kids loved swimming in the kidney-shaped pool, and also off beaches in Cricieth and Llanbedrog. We had a slap-up meal in Castell Deudraeth on our last evening, finishing with a cake bearing the crossed flags of Wales and Cyprus. We were transported to and from the hotel on what looked like golf-carts. And absolutely no food poisoning. We even still have the splendid plate that bore our cake. Though don't tell Portmeirion.

Conclusion

So, while my Welshness seemed at the time on the verge of extinction after a half-century's exile in England, it has since become apparent to me, crouched as I am beneath extinction's alp, that it was dormant, not dead.

It just needed something to nudge it awake. More of which in the next chapter.

Part Four

Our Annus Mirabilis

No, it's nothing to do with buttocks or rear ends, miraculous or otherwise – that extra 'n' is very important. This is the concept of a 'marvellous year'. For Hollywood, it was 1939 – the year of *The Wizard of Oz*, *Gone with the Wind* and *Wuthering Heights*. For American presidents it was 1946 – the only year in history in which three presidents were born: Trump, Bush and Clinton. For football it was 1972: the birth year of three winners of the Ballon d'Or: Zidane, Rivaldo, Figo.

For my relationship with Wales, my annus mirabilis was 2022:

1. The posting on Facebook of memories about growing up in Pwllheli from 2019 onwards led to their collection into a book which was published in 2022.

2. The decision on my part and that of my wife that what we really needed was not a series of temporary stays in campsites all over Wales, but a settled base in the north which we could visit and revisit in the autumn of our years. Leading, in 2022, to the purchase of a static caravan in Llanddulas.

3. A remarkable confluence of events that came about towards the end of August 2022.

CHAPTER 14

On Bonfires, Butlins and Being Welsh

As I MENTIONED in the Introduction, this current book arose from, and is a sequel to, my first – *On Bonfires, Butlins and Being Welsh*. Although it was about Wales, although it was published by a leading Welsh publisher – Y Lolfa – it was, I'm sorry to say, written in English. My Welsh just wasn't up to the job.

That original book came out in April 2022 – a compilation of Facebook posts and the comments they provoked which conjured up a picture of what it was like to grow up in Pwllheli in the 1950s and '60s.

Though I'd written guidebooks (to Croatia, to the Greek Islands, to Yorkshire, to Cyprus), this was what I considered to be my first *real* book. I was cock-a-hoop. I anticipated, with barely suppressed euphoria, demands for interviews from the world's press, approaches from Steven Spielberg for the film rights, and from Mark Zuckerberg thanking me (tearfully) for my positive attitude to his brainchild Facebook which was at that time going through a rough patch.

Pride, of course, comes before a fall. My phone remained silent, my inbox filled only with spam. Though my editor assured me that they must all have lost my contact details, I couldn't help feeling a bit miffed, a bit *ceg gam*, as we say in Wales.

Although the world in general responded with total indifference, I was delighted by Welsh interest in the book:

- Though writers of international best-sellers would no doubt scoff, I was chuffed with the sales of 600 copies in the first six months. For a while it was outselling the Harry Potter books. At least in Pwllheli's Gaol Street bookshop. Eat your heart out, J K Rowling!

- A book signing in that shop, organised by proprietor Steve Wright, kept me busy for a whole morning, chatting and exchanging memories with people I'd not seen since my teens.

- I was interviewed (twice) on Radio Wales, and was invited to write an article for Wales International's newsletter *Yr Enfys*.

- Above all, I was able to reconnect with the people of my home town online, by Facebook post and in person, after more than fifty years in England.

- Good-will messages flooded in from friends who I knew in those far-off days, from relatives of friends who appeared in the book – Garnett's widow and all three sisters, sisters too of Mop and Jonesy, Brian's wife (who also helped look after my mother in her later years), people who knew Joe, the daughters of two of our teachers (Maldwyn and Brasso), and of two of the guys I worked with on the boats at Butlins (Dick Parry and Bill McGill). John Cholomondely's sister got in touch to say that her brother would be very proud that he'd got a mention. I was pleased to hear it – I'd seen rumours online that he was no longer with us. I'd pictured God on his celestial throne patiently listening to John's list of the places he'd visited on his way to heaven.

- I've since heard that John has finally passed on, to an extraordinary outpouring in the town of affection and grief.

- Two messages particularly delighted me:

  o The first was from Nan (Roberts that was) from Llithfaen, who had been in my class in school and who contacted me from Cardiff, where she now lives, to say that she has no memory at all of hiding my maths book in her desk to save me from Maldwyn's wrath. But she does remember a message that I left at her Bedford College hall of residence during our first year at London University (I was at LSE), to the effect that I'd called, but that she was out. I, in turn, have no memory whatsoever of my visit, never mind of leaving her a message. Throughout writing the two books, I've been constantly reminded of how unreliable memory can be.

  o The second was from the daughter of Williams 80, the grocery shop used by my parents throughout their lives in Pwllheli. I'd mentioned (and I'm so glad that I did!) that she was very pretty, that my brother Jeff really fancied her, but that her father had stopped her going out with him because he thought he was a bad influence, a ne'er-do-well, a 'teddy boy'. And who's to blame him? Her message told me that, yes, her father had disapproved, but that she had secretly defied him and dated Jeff. At least for a while. She now lives in Canada, and has loads of children and grandchildren.

- I've also been in touch with one of my older brother Jeff's mates (John Prys) who was able to fill me in on details to which I wasn't party at the time, and which he hadn't told me at Jeff's funeral. All these years I've thought that Jeff's friends had just dumped him on our doorstep after his fall from the gasometer. Not so, John informed me. They'd wanted to call an ambulance, but he'd insisted that they take him home, that he was OK. I should explain that Jeff didn't die of the fall, though he might well have done. No, his funeral was forty years later, so no lasting harm was done at the time.

- A letter from my cousin Christine in south Wales corrected my spelling of the Italian café in Ferndale – Fecce's, not Fessies. In my defence I'd never seen it written down. And I'm not Italian.

- Finally, I was particularly delighted to receive two lovely written messages of appreciation – a card and a letter (old school or what?) which were passed on to me by the publisher. One was from David Griffiths who used to play golf with my dad and now lives in Cardiff. The other was from Mair Lloyd Davies, the wife of a local Non-conformist minister. When she and her husband lived in Ala Road, they knew Dad and the three Macbeth's witches – Mum, Auntie Eva and Auntie Annie May – and also their neighbours Dafydd Bodlew and his family, and Mr and Mrs Martin and their brood. All mentioned in the book. Had I realised, when I was writing the book that the wife of a minister would read it, I'd have moderated my language and perhaps left out some of the anecdotes. Not, I've a feeling, that she was worried – she seemed very down to earth. She even suggested that my survival into old age is a tribute to the preservative qualities of alcohol. In my day, chapel people weren't known for a sense of humour regarding the demon drink! I was very appreciative, especially as it's not often these days that I hear from people who are even older than myself. It was clear, too, that our memories of life in mid twentieth-century Llŷn stirred *hiraeth* in Llŷnites (if there is such a word) all over the world, from China to Australia and Denmark to California to Greece, where members of the north Wales diaspora had read the book and felt that bit closer to home.

NB. If some of the above is difficult to follow, you really need to read the original book (*On Bonfires, Butlins and Being Welsh*), still available from the publisher Y Lolfa, and from all good bookshops, real and online. As I've probably mentioned before.

CHAPTER 15

Our little welsh home in the west

SINCE MY WIFE and I have been campers and caravanners for most of our married lives, the obvious way of reconnecting with Wales was to explore it using campsites for our accommodation. This we did, as I've already mentioned, from Harlech to Cardiff to St Davids, Betws-y-Coed to Bala to Barmouth. We even took in border towns by visiting the Hay Festival, and, for a while at least, followed in the footsteps of George Borrow.

Slowly, though, we concluded that what we wanted was not an itinerant exploration of the whole of Wales, but a relationship with an area which was easily accessible from where we lived, was interesting, was close to the sea, and which perhaps had a connection with my family. Quite a few boxes to tick. Llŷn was too far away, the mid Wales coast around Harlech involved too many miles of narrow roads used by psychopathic tractor drivers, and Rhyl, Prestatyn and points east were (sorry about this) too Anglicised.

The place we found ourselves returning to more and more often was the Conwy/Bae Colwyn/Llandudno/Abergele area. It ticked all those boxes.

Its accessibility couldn't be faulted – an hour and a half's drive from our home in north Staffordshire, all on motorway and dual carriageway. And the campsite which we found most convenient, Bron-y-Wendon in Llanddulas, was just off the North Wales Expressway.

The touring site was very well run and overlooked the sea. The village had a lovely little pub, a good Indian restaurant, a fine fish and chip shop (now alas closed), and a twenty-four-hour garage which, in addition to petrol, dispensed an encouraging variety of alcoholic drinks. There was even the little Afon Dulas at the bottom of the hill in which our granddaughter could paddle and flip stones.

And, as for family connections, these were the cherries on the cake:

- Llanddulas (or possibly Old Colwyn) was, so my mother once informed me before she died (well it would have been, wouldn't it?) where *her* father, my grandfather, was born and brought up. And it certainly seemed likely – he was a stonemason, and virtually the only employer in Llanddulas was the quarry. He left for south Wales in search of work, and I'm really glad he did – otherwise, I wouldn't exist. And neither, of course, would my siblings, my children or my grandchildren. His house in the Rhondda he named 'Colwyn House', and one of his sons was christened 'Colwyn'. My own son is probably glad I didn't follow the same pattern, otherwise he'd be, not Daniel, but Pwllheli. Bit of a mouthful in Dubai.

- Furthermore, on my mother's side both great-grandparents and all four great-great-grandparents were from this part of north Wales. Something that I discovered, thanks to the endeavours of my mate Steve.

- Llandudno was not only one of the destinations for Sunday school trips when I was a kid, but where I went to a Beatles gig in 1963.

- Finally, my father died in Llandudno Junction in 1974, on the way to see a north Wales XV take on a Tongan touring side in Rhyl. OK, not a cause for celebration, but certainly a connection.

In due course, though, even camping in Llanddulas wasn't enough. We wanted somewhere more permanent. But that was the problem. We could, no doubt, have scraped together enough money to buy a small flat in, say, Llandudno, or a cottage in one of north Wales's villages. There were plenty on Rightmove and Zoopla. But there were also stories in the national press about the way in which second homes, holiday lets and Airbnbs were destroying villages in north Wales. Abersoch for example, near where I was brought up. How could we, in all conscience, add to the problem by helping to price local people out of a home?

That's when fate took a hand. I received an e-mail from Bron-y-Wendon campsite saying that they had a second-hand static caravan for sale. We hadn't even realised that Bron-y-Wendon *had* static vans. We booked a pitch on the touring park, drove over to Llanddulas in our VW camper, and had a look.

The static was luxurious. It had central heating, two bedrooms and bathrooms, a fully-fitted kitchen, and a big fridge that could hold huge amounts of beer and wine. And with a deck that overlooked the sea and the Gwynt-y-Môr wind farm, one of the biggest in the world. Together with spectacular sunsets. What was not to like? We loved it.

Within a fortnight we'd sold the campervan and bought the static. We now had a permanent place to stay in north Wales.

Beyond Llanddulas, the local area lay at our feet – the stunning triumvirate of Llandudno, Bae Colwyn and Conwy. Three totally different towns, all less than half an hour from us by car.

Our impressions of the area around Llanddulas, arrived at during our first few months in the area, were very positive. I'll outline them from notes I wrote at the time.

Bae Colwyn

Closest to us was Bae Colwyn, or as we Pwllheli Sunday school trippers knew it, Colwyn Bay.

We loved:

- Driving to Hen Colwyn (Old Colwyn) just down the road from Llanddulas – a hill, a couple of huge, and hugely impressive quarries gouged out of the hillside, and a long main street.

- Swooping down the North Wales Expressway, past the Llanddulas quarry pier and under the rainbow bridge (so-called for its shape, not its colour). We never tired of the view – the sea in all its moods, the headland, the Gwynt-y-Môr wind turbines waving to us from out near the horizon. 'It reminds me of the South of France,' I said the first time, expecting a disbelieving guffaw from my wife. None came – she totally agreed. OK, we could have done without Morrisons and the fifty-mile-an-hour speed limit, but it's a ride that never failed to lift our spirits.

- On our way to Llandudno, we would usually take the slip-road down onto the eastern end of Bae Colwyn's prom, to enjoy the road along next to the beach, past Porth Eirias, through Llandrillo-yn-Rhos (Rhos-on-Sea), and out towards Rhos's lovely new promenade and the Little Orme. Rhos was a picture when the tide was in – people on the beach, boats bobbing in the little harbour, just enough places to buy fishing nets and buckets and spades. Very 1950s.

- The new 20mph speed limit at first seemed a bit of a pain, but I grew to like it – plenty of time to look around! Even now, though, it does seem awfully slow.

- The Welsh Mountain Zoo was a big hit with our granddaughter, though the tigers refused to do their stuff, skulking out of sight in the vegetation. She had to make do with the occasional roar.

- And the beach! Must be one of the best in the world. Eat your hearts out Llandudno and Conwy. Even Bondi (Australia) and Venice (USA). Lots of parking, beautifully updated promenade, a (curiously) truncated pier that doesn't reach the sea, distances marked out for joggers, ample toilets and places to buy drinks and ice-creams, and miles and miles (and miles) of sand.

- Bae Colwyn town itself was, we thought, a bit sad the first time we drove through it. Like almost every other town outside the south-east of England. But look carefully, and there are lots of good things to enjoy – interesting independent shops, little cafés, nice Victorian glass and iron arcades, Theatr Colwyn. Why it needs quite so many churches and chapels I'm not sure – in the past the town must have had a lot to ask the Lord's forgiveness for.

- We haven't tried Porth Eirias Park yet. We asked friends if they'd like to join us for a Rag 'n' Bone Man gig there, but they couldn't make it. So we didn't go. They did come for New Year's Eve, had a meal at the Little Indian Chef restaurant and watched Llandudno's fireworks from the deck of the static. The next morning, we had breakfast at Bryn Williams's at Porth Eirias, and watched the New Year's Day swimmers plunging into the sea. We admired their fortitude. No, I tell a lie. We thought they were mad.

Llandudno

We loved Llandudno for so, so many reasons:
- The obvious ones are that it's a stunningly beautiful and superior resort, much favoured by the Victorian and Edwardian middle-class and, more recently, its haughtily superior goats. Though also, alas, marauding herring gulls. We love walking along the prom beside the

great crescent of stately hotels, or out along the pier. We stop for tea or lunch, often at the St George Hotel.

- It's a brilliant shopping centre. Town planners have kept the big stores we all disparage but love to patronise separate from, but within easy walking distance of, the centre of the town. And with ample parking. Whoever these planners were, we salute you.

- A lot of visitors to Llandudno are like us – long in the tooth. Feeling our age. Have seen better days. But we're amply catered for – Llandudno must be the public-bench capital of the world. I really do find this a godsend, because I am ambulatorily challenged. I can only walk for a limited time, and only stand for even less. But in Llandudno, with my trusty smart-phone in my pocket and a book or two in the backpack slung over my shoulder, I'm up for hours of sitting on the prom or outside shops, waiting for my wife, who has a great deal more stamina than I have. Though she's six months younger. Wait till she gets to my age.

- When our fourteen-year-old granddaughter is staying with us in Llanddulas, we've developed a routine for our trips into Llandudno, which includes:
  o A visit to Waterstones, where I can have a coffee upstairs (there's a lift), she can choose as many books as she likes, and my wife can queue at the till and pay for them.
  o Shopping in the cat charity shop on Mostyn Street, where she always manages to find really stylish clothes at knock-down prices.
  o Crêpes at Fortes.

- Other less regular pleasures (in fact just the once in each case) have included:
  o The Great Orme Copper Mines which, somewhat to our surprise, she loved.

- o A show at Venue Cymru (sure to become a regular event in future).
- And, when we were in Llandudno on our own:
  - o A round trip around the Great Orme on Marine Drive. With spectacular views across the sea to the mountains of Eryri.
  - o A visit to the small injuries clinic at Llandudno Hospital. When the end bit of my wife's hearing aid came off and lodged itself in her ear canal. It had to be removed by a nurse with a pair of tweezers. Not very rock and roll, you might think, and not much of a 'pleasure'. But leaving it in there would have been, in the long run, even less pleasurable.
  - o Wax removal from both of my ears in a shop-front clinic in Mostyn Street. A procedure, the attractive young woman who wielded the suction device told me, might well be necessary again in future. 'How is that a pleasure?' I hear you ask. But I wouldn't have heard you ask it if I hadn't had the wax removed. Again, not very rock and roll, but, as Bette Davies said, old age is not for cissies.

Conwy

Whereas I had happy memories of Llandudno and Colwyn Bay from childhood Sunday school trips, the only memories of Conwy that I could excavate were of long traffic queues and choking petrol fumes. What a change the North Wales Expressway and the tunnel have made to the town.

The view of Conwy, its castle and walls, its estuary and harbour, and its background of green hills as you drive across one of its bridges must be among the most beautiful in the UK. Too good to be true I muttered, as we threaded our way along to the car park in Castle Street. But it's not – Conwy is quite as beautiful as it looks at a distance. The town is still hugged by its walls, and you come across crenelated masonry and towers wherever you look. The quayside, with its moored boats, piles of lobsterpots, and kids fishing for crabs, is remarkably unspoilt. The quayside pub – the Liverpool Arms – is an old-fashioned inn, dedicated to liquid rather than solid refreshment, and cool and dark on a hot summer's day. Even the understated smallest house in Britain, with its lady in Welsh costume outside, and the small group of funfair rides, doesn't feel at all exploitative. Tea at the Jester's Tower (great views of the estuary, really excellent cheese toasties), visits to the Knight shop (you can't miss it – there's a full-size suit of armour standing guard outside), wandering the narrow, busy streets, specialist shops (the Cheese Room, the Clock Shop), bread and pies from Dylan's, meals or snacks at L's Coffee & Bookshop, strolls upriver along Marine Walk towards the big secondary school – Conwy has become one of our favourite days out. And how many small towns can have a railway station smack in the centre without spoiling its atmosphere, or a splendid parish church right in the middle, a haven of peacefully tranquillity with a grave associated with Wordsworth?

Those are the highlights of our first year in Llanddulas. Add the Welsh Food Centre, Bodnant Gardens, Happy Valley, and the whole hinterland that we have yet to explore – the mountains of Eryri, Sir Fôn, and the lands and villages between us and the English border – Wrexham, Holywell, Denbigh, Mold. Not to mention my own old stamping ground in the far west – Llŷn.

That should be enough to keep us occupied until we shuffle off this mortal coil, hopefully to join the choir invisible.

CHAPTER 16

A confluence
of events

OUR PURCHASE OF the static caravan in Llanddulas was almost immediately followed by a confluence of events which, in spectacular fashion, confirmed and enhanced my return to the bosom of the Celtic fringe. If fringes have bosoms.

I think this part of the tale might best be told as a fairy story – it certainly has a mythic quality.

A Tale of Two Chums

Once upon a time (in 1964), two local lads left Pwllheli, the town which had nurtured them from birth, to seek their fortune – two stalwarts, stout cudgels resting on their shoulders, their earthly possessions wrapped in a spotted neckerchief tied to the end, striding eastwards towards England and the rising sun, their shadows streaming back westwards towards Wales and home. Like an art deco poster from the 1920s.

Tony Pierce (for he was one) was embarking on a pre-diploma course at Liverpool College of Art. In Liverpool. Jos Simon (for he was the other) was to study for a BSc (Econ) at the London School of Economics. In London.

The two chums kept in touch, at least for a while. They visited one another in their respective great cities. In Pwllheli, too, they hooked up for raucous nights out during the holidays. Or 'vacations', as they now felt compelled to call them.

Tony moved on to a three-year course in stained glass at Swansea College of Art. Jos finished at LSE with 'the boozer's degree' (Third Class Honours) and proceeded to a Postgraduate Certificate in Education at a college in south London. Still they kept in touch. They each got married – Tony to a Spanish girl, Jos to a Greek Cypriot. They each had two children, a boy and a girl. Or at least their wives did.

Moving to France, Tony set up his own business translating documents for NATO. Jos wasn't sure how this came about – interpreting defence documents would not seem an obvious career progression from working in stained glass. Jos became a teacher, in various parts of England – an obvious career progression, given that his father, his older brother, his sister-in-law, his uncle and aunt, his wife (and indeed, eventually, his children) all were, or were to become, teachers. This shows dedication. Or, it's true, a lack of imagination.

Jos's younger brother, having initially failed to resist the siren call of teaching, came to his senses just in time and joined the civil service.

In due course, though, there came the inevitable parting of the ways. The last time they met was when Jos, his wife and two children visited Tony and *his* wife in Paris. Tony's children were elsewhere – I think with their grandparents – which allowed Jos's kids to sleep in Tony's kids' beds. (*'I now sleep in that bed'*, Tony's granddaugher Emma later told Jos, but that's jumping ahead of the story.) All this was some time in the 1980s – Jos's daughter Catherine, who is blessed with a photographic memory for family holidays, will remember the exact date.

Tony and Jos stayed in sporadic contact – though only online. In due course they gravitated to the same Facebook groups, especially *Ysgolion Pwllheli and District Schools* and *Old Pictures of Pwllheli*. When Jos started posting memories of his Pwllheli upbringing, Tony started to pitch in with always pertinent, sometimes impertinent and invariably sarcastic comments. He pointed out that he'd never been paid a fee for his consultancy when decorating Jos's bedroom in Llŷn Street. And (a bombshell this) he put up a photograph of a *Little Oxford Dictionary* (Jos's *Little Oxford Dictionary*), gleefully pointing out the title page where it's original, and rightful, owner's name and address (J Ll Simon, Llys Pedr, Lleyn Street, Pwllheli, Caerns, Wales, Britain, Europe, The World, the Solar System, the Milky Way, the Universe) had been crossed out and his own substituted. 'So that's where it went!' Jos cried when he saw the post. 'He's stolen/pinched/pilfered/half-inched/purloined it!' (He may have lost his dictionary, but he still owned a Thesaurus.) 'The thieving bastard!'

Tony posted contributions of his own. They included detailed accounts of aspects of his life as a child and a teenager in Pwllheli (on swimming, for example), and philosophical musings about the passage of time. He complained about having been forced, as not only the oldest member of his group of friends ('the boys') but the only one with both a driving licence and a car, to become their chauffeur during comprehensive underage explorations of Llŷn Peninsula pubs. On Messenger he made threats of legal action ('…if you write a book, I'm gonna sue'), and sent Jos a stream of scurrilous anecdotes that couldn't possibly, for legal reasons, be posted on Facebook. Or indeed included in this book. He confirmed, too, what Jos had long suspected – that he, Tony, was blessed with the luck of the devil. One of his Swansea professors suspected that, if Tony fell into the harbour, he'd climb out, not only unharmed, but with his pockets full of fish.

It seemed that the friendship of these two chums, separated by many miles, many years and Brexit, was destined to fade gently into a geriatric sunset. But it was not to be.

To return to real-time, and the confluence of events:

Out of a clear blue sky, Tony, that school-chum from all

those years ago, wondered on Facebook if any member of *Ysgolion Pwllheli and District Schools* might be interested in hosting his twelve-year-old granddaughter for a couple of weeks in the summer so that she could improve her English. Ideally, he added, with a family which contained a daughter of roughly the same age. Could he have been aiming this request at me, I wondered? The tinker!

Before I could even mention the possibility to my own daughter, it was all done and dusted. Catherine in Newcastle-under-Lyme had seen the post, had been in touch with Ifan (Tony's son) in Spain. Emma (Ifan's daughter, Tony's granddaugter – aged twelve) would be flying to the UK, to be hosted by Arianwen (my granddaughter – aged twelve) and her family. As that great (if flawed) Welshman Tommy Cooper said, 'Just like that'. And if you're finding this hard to follow, do pay attention.

Emma arrived at Manchester Airport. A few days later she, Arianwen and Arianwen's family set off for Nefyn, where they'd booked accommodation for a week. They walked on the beach and along part of the north Wales coastal path. They climbed Yr Eifl. They scaled Yr Wyddfa (and not, be it noted, on the train).

Meanwhile, I, my wife and my son Daniel had signed in at the Lion Hotel in Cricieth.

Now I need to say a word about my son Daniel. A teacher in Dubai, he usually came home twice each year – at Christmas and during the summer. The family usually celebrated his birthday in some way (a meal, a short holiday), but couldn't do so on his actual birthday (towards the end of August) because it always fell after he'd returned to the Middle East. Bearing in mind that the family meeting in Nefyn took place in August 2022, and that Dan was born in August 1972, the arithmetically gifted will realise the significance of the dates. Yes, Daniel was due a short holiday and a meal to celebrate his birthday. And not any old birthday – his fiftieth!

We all – us from Cricieth, the rest from Nefyn – met up in Pwllheli. I spent a day dragging the girls – my granddaughter and Tony's granddaughter – around the town, taking pictures of them outside places that had featured in my and Tony's childhood. The backdrops to this fashion-shoot were:

o Barma's rock shop (as was) in the Maes.

o Tony's family house (then the Bank Place Hotel) at 29–31 High Street.

o My family house (then Llys Pedr) at 14 Llŷn Street.

o Penlleiniau, where my dad had been the headteacher, where I and my two brothers were educated, and where my dad and my mum eventually lived (and where mum continued to live after Dad's death) in the school house.

o The Liberal Club where we'd played snooker.

o The Town Hall where 'the boys' went to the pictures, and once where Tony, the only one, at sixteen legally old enought to watch the X-rated film, was the only one to be challenged by the usherette collecting the tickets. How we all laughed. Except Tony.

o The Penlan Fawr where on occasion we would enjoy a pint. Or even two. Only after we were eighteen of course. Otherwise, being local, our underagedness would have been recognised, and we'd have been kicked out.

o Gimblet Rock and the Beach Café.

The two girls put up with this with remarkable fortitude. Though, I've got to admit, an undercurrent of resentment.

Then, in the evening:

• We all met in Nefyn for a meal at the Nanhoron Arms Hotel. A great evening during which:

o Emma, with impeccable timing, produced the very dictionary stolen sixty years before from me by her grandfather Tony. The felon had put her up to this.

- o Emma also confided that she never believed anything her grandfather told her, except when he said that she should never believe anything that I told her. The minx.

- o Daniel was embarassed by the appearance of a cake and the singing of 'Happy Birthday' by the whole restaurant. They're a friendly bunch in Nefyn. Emma cut the cake with great aplomb. And also with a knife, the handle of which fell off.

- o After the meal, we all strolled along the cliff-top path above Nefyn beach. The sun was setting spectacularly beyond Porthdinllaen, the muted splashing of the few remaining holiday-makers paddling/swimming/canoeing far below drifted up, and the whole scene was of gentle and surpassing beauty. I wondered why I ever left Llŷn.

- You see what I meant by a confluence of events:
  - o In the autumn of 1964 Tony and I had set off from the Llŷn Peninsula to seek our fortune. Unencumbered by wives, children, money or any sense of responsibility.
  - o Fifty-eight years later, Tony's son's daughter and my daughter's daughter (and indeed my wife, my son, my daughter's two other children, together with my son-in-law), met back on the Llŷn Peninsula, a confluence arranged by Tony's son and my daughter. The circle was complete.

During the celebrations in Nefyn, I had a vision of the future:

- Of Emma and Arianwen staying in touch, even of becoming besties (I've always prided myself on keeping up with the youth vernacular).

- Of them visiting each other in England and Spain, perhaps eventually attending university in each other's countries.

- Of, maybe, Tony and I and our wives meeting up for a few bevvies and reminiscences. Of Ifan and Catherine's two families keeping in touch.

Then it got darker.

- Of Tony at my funeral.
- Or, more likely, of me at Tony's funeral. He *is* nearly a year older than I am. Though I think he's considerably fitter.

With, needless to say, the families of one or the other, or even both, sobbing at their loss.

Speculation rather than memoir, true. But we can all dream!

Part Five

A Temporary Welshman

As if the confluence of events I wrote about in the last chapter were not enough of an omen, in October 2022 we put our house in Newcastle-under-Lyme on the market, looking to downsize. To life on one level. Yes, a bungalow. We're both approaching eighty – it comes to us all in the end. If we're lucky.

The sale went through, and we had to vacate by 1 March 2023. Significantly, St David's Day.

- We'd found a house that we really liked, a dormer-bungalow. However, there was a down-side – the owners couldn't vacate until 1 September. On the plus side, it was originally owned by Stanley Matthews's daughter. At last – a real if tenuous claim to fame of my own!

- This left us with a gap of six months, during which we had to live in our (thank God we bought it) static caravan in Llanddulas. Had to! It was a pleasure!

Six months! Six months, spanning spring and summer, with nothing to do but sit on the deck, look at the sea, enjoy the sunsets and get to know the area.

Bliss!

I started to reconnect with being Welsh, full of good intentions but with no hint of a plan. The elephant in the room was my imperfect command of the language. If I was really committed to reconnecting with my roots, surely the minimum I should do was to brush up (or at least give the kiss of life to) my Welsh. But when you're approaching eighty, it starts to seem a bit pointless – how much longer was I likely to grace the world with my presence? And surely St Peter speaks English. Or has an interpreter.

I decided to say goodbye to self-contempt, and just do the best I could.

Apart from bare necessities, all our 'stuff' was in storage. The static took ten minutes to clean, the campsite was responsible for cutting the grass, and despite a fully functioning kitchen, we tended to live off take-aways and microwave meals. Live the dream!

I had a clear six months to try to plug into the north Wales zeitgeist. My efforts might have been a bit random, but I loved them all.

CHAPTER 17

The *Daily Post*'s online 'North Wales Live'

I SIGNED UP for the *Daily Post*'s 'North Wales Live' newsletter. Immediately, avalanches of news about north Wales poured into my inbox. This was interesting:

- A lot of it was about north-east Wales, a not very glamorous area and one that I didn't know at all. Before Ryan Reynolds and his mate bought Wrexham, of course. But it made me determined to explore it.

- A huge amount of it was about my adopted home area – Bae Colwyn /Llandudno/Conwy.

- More than I expected was about the beautiful place where I grew up – Llŷn.

Of course, the *Daily Post* is no different from any other regional paper. It tends to concentrate on court and police reports, business news and so on. Therefore, the picture it presents seems to be, shall we say, biased towards the sensational. Yet I'd have to admit that I really enjoy the coverage – I think they do a great job. So far:

- I know a lot more already than I did about Fflint, Mold, Holywell, Denbigh, Wrexham and others, and became determined to use our base in Llanddulas to explore these unfashionable but really interesting places.

- I've had heads-ups about changes in the shops in Llandudno, about flooding in Llanrwst, about a mysterious empty boat that fetched up on the beach between the pier and Porth Eirias in Bae Colwyn, and a lot more than I need to know about crashes on the A55. How long before we get a headline 'No crashes or holdups on the North Wales Expressway?'

- Who knew that the eastern part of the beach in Cricieth is being eroded? Or that an air ambulance had to take somebody – the victim of a crash between Penrhos and Llanbedrog – to hospital in Liverpool? Or that a 70-year-old Brummie lives on £25 a week in a converted lorry in Porthmadog? Or about the continuing debate about incomers pricing locals out of the housing market? Or that *'carreg y bwgan'*, haunted by the ghost of a headless man and even the devil himself, keeps witches trapped underneath Anglesey? Or that South Stack lighthouse is also haunted – by the ghost of previous lighthouse-keeper Jack Jones? Or that a ferocious debate has broken out about using Welsh rather than English place-names: Eryri rather than Snowdonia, Yr Wyddfa rather than Snowdon, Caerdydd rather than Cardiff? Or (shock, horror!) that the introduction of a 20mph speed limit in built-up areas is not universally welcomed.

If there's one single thing that has eased me back into north Walian life, it's the *Daily Post*. Many, many thanks!

CHAPTER 18

Welsh music

WHEN LOOKING AT ways of getting in touch with recent Welsh music, I came across a two-part BBC programme, *Wales: Music Nation with Huw Stephens*. It introduced me to several strands of Welsh music – the well-trodden world of male-voice choirs and Welsh-language pop/rock/folk music, but also the byways of the music of church and chapel, of harp and crwth. Even Rap. I'd be very grateful if music buffs in the group could point out any mistakes I've made (my excuse is total ignorance) or add anything that deserves to be added.

To start with, the programme set so many hares running that I tied myself up in a welter of Google and Wikipedia knots trying to follow them all. In due course, though, it provided me with the beginnings of a road map for exploring Welsh music which will probably last me to the end of this life and well into the next.

It started with rock/pop, where at least I'd heard of some of the names – The Manic Street Preachers, the Super Furry Animals, the Stereophonics, Gorky's Psychotic Monkey, Catatonia. And Duffy, of course – she's from Nefyn, just down the road from where I was brought up. Others too that I hadn't come across before, among them Gwenno and Cate le Bon.

Then there was Folk – old-school Sain stalwarts like Dafydd Iwan. Meic Stevens and Y Chwyldro, young guns like Calan, VRï and Plu.

I continued to learn about Welsh music, but still within my

comfort zone. The Treorchy Male Voice Choir, 'Cwm Rhondda', 'Hen Wlad fy Nhadau' and Caradog's (Griffith Rhys Jones) Côr Mawr. But I was soon out of my depth with hymn-writer Ann Griffiths and the rarified world of Tudor/Stuart madrigal composer Thomas Tomkins and the antiphon, the music of Nansi Richards and the triple harp, of 'Carys' Meurig and the crwth.

I'd never heard of Morfydd Llwyn Owen, a great Welsh composer who died tragically at the age of 26, or even Sir Karl Jenkins CBE, probably the most performed living composer in the world, whose music I'd heard many times over the years but whose name I'd never come across. Just over two years older than myself, he looks like the kind of guy you might find yourself sitting next to at the bar in the Con Club. If it wasn't now a dental practice.

Finally, Rap. Who knew that there was an infant Rap scene in Wales? I was introduced to Mace the Great, a rapper based in Splott. Not a sentence I ever expected to write. I know nothing about Rap, but I rather liked his featured song.

Before leaving this round-up of my Welsh musical ignorance, I'd like to mention Canu'r Pwnc. No, not the Welsh version of punk, though Llygod Ffyrnig were name-checked as the first Welsh punk band, but an odd, religiously-inspired community activity.

I'd never heard of Canu'r Pwnc, and it appears to have left behind very few recordings. It seems to be a strange and ancient harmonised chanting of passages from the Bible. It exists (or existed) in south-west Wales. It could go on, apparently, for a whole weekend, with people from different villages joining and leaving as time went on – a bit like a two-day football match with unlimited substitutes. But the sound is extraordinary, fit to set the hairs on the back of your neck lifting. Google it – there are a couple of examples out there.

The All Blacks have their Maori chant. But I reckon that, if the Welsh team faced them on the field of battle with Canu'r Pwnc, they'd blast the haka out of the park!

201

Welsh Music – postscript

Comments arising from this post were wide-ranging.

1. Some were very welcome corrections – it wasn't 'Carys' but 'Cass' Meurig.

2. Others were castigations for leaving out a variety of well-known Welsh songsters – Tom Jones, Shirley Bassey, John Cale, Shakin' Stevens. My only excuse – they are so famously Welsh that I didn't think they were worth mentioning. As for Max Boyce, I understand that he can be an acquired taste, but he often left me helpless with laughter. And like many Welsh national figures, he has stayed admirably true to his roots.

3. As I should perhaps have expected, the post led to a deluge of names put forward by fans taking up the cudgels on behalf of their favourite local band. I Googled each one, and have to admit that the standard was high:

   - Feeder
   - Catfish and the Bottlemen
   - Pino Palladino
   - Huw Jones singing 'Dŵr'
   - Man Band
   - Budgie
   - Iorwerth Pritchard and the Neutrons
   - Love Sculpture
   - Bwncath (with Elidyr Glyn from Llanllyfni)
   - 'Fel Hyn 'da ni Fod'
   - Edward H Dafis

4. I have to admit too that, at times, I felt that some of these names had been invented just to wind me up. The final straw came when I was told off (by my own brother) for not mentioning Y Tebot Piws. The Purple Teapot! Please! When I challenged him ('Come clean – you made that up') I was directed by him to an entry in Welsh Wicipedia, and by somebody else to a YouTube clip. Not only did they exist, but they aren't half bad!

5. Finally, my mention of Welsh 'Rap' led to a spirited debate on the merits, or otherwise, of Rap as a musical genre. But I stick to my guns – I liked Mace the Great. And who can argue with a rapper from Splott?

CHAPTER 19

'The Literary Map of Wales'

MY WIFE BOUGHT me a copy of the 'Literary Map of Wales' (Map Llenorion Cymru) for my birthday. I was hoping for a Ferrari, but you can't have everything. And it was brilliant – a single scroll of paper which promised hours of future enjoyment, of research and travel. The map covers the whole of Wales, with the names of prominent literary figures entered in the geographical areas with which they're mainly associated. This could be the key to future exploration – reading-up about the writers, then travelling to see their stomping grounds.

The obvious place to start was where I was born and bred – the Llŷn Peninsula. I was amazed, and chastened, to discover that I'd never heard of most of the names that covered Llŷn.

Time to put that right, I thought.

William Llŷn

All I (or indeed anyone) can say about William Llŷn is that he was born in Llŷn. The clue's in the bardic name which, apparently, he chose for himself. Though how they know it wasn't simply his surname I've no idea – his brother was Huw Llŷn, his children Jane and Richard Llŷn. And I can't pin down where he actually entered this world either. Not a good start.

He was born, it's thought, in 1534 or 1535, and based on

what a fellow-poet said (that he was 'not yet forty-six' when he died) he departed this life in 1580ish.

He was, according to those who know, the last great Welsh poet of the medieval bardic tradition and is regarded as possibly the most eminent of the Welsh elegists. This, of course, means little if you know nothing about the bardic tradition, and if you wouldn't know an elegist if he bit you on the bum. Certainly true of me when I first read his Wikipedia entry.

Further research informed me that:

- The medieval bardic tradition was common, not only to Wales, but to Scotland, Ireland, Cornwall and Brittany.
- Bards were professional poets employed to write elegies for medieval lords.
- The tradition was revived in the eighteenth century with the development of the eisteddfod movement.

When I proceeded to read up about the intricacies of modern eisteddfodau, I noticed that my will to live was ebbing away, so I decided to stop. If you want to know more, I'm afraid you're on your own.

To get back to William Llŷn. As one of the *beirdd yr uchelwyr* (poets of the nobility), he composed poems on commission for Welsh aristocrats all over north and mid Wales. To quote two modern aphorisms, he knew which side his bread was buttered on and he didn't bite the hand that fed him. So the poems were very complimentary, and his patrons really liked them. Well, they would, wouldn't they?

William moved to Oswestry (in those days a Welsh-speaking town, despite being in England) in his thirties, ended his life's journey there, and was buried in its churchyard, though nobody knows where.

Just like his birth, really.

I'm not competent to judge the quality of his work, but he must have been good at his job: he got excellent write-ups from Welsh poets who came after him, and two of his poems were included in the *Oxford Book of Welsh Verse*.

Ceridwen Peris

When researching Ceridwen Peris (the pseudonym of Alice Gray Jones 1852–1943), I immediately hit a snag. There didn't seem to be any agreement over where she was born. One source said Trefor, another Llanllyfni. I'd have settled for Trefor, since that puts her well within the Llŷn Peninsula, but her family seemed all to be from the Llanberis area (hence the name Ceridwen *Peris*), and even when claiming that she was born in Trefor, it said 'Trefor, near Llanberis'. At twenty miles apart, 'near' is a bit of a stretch. So perhaps there's another Trefor hidden in the mountains of Eryri, though I couldn't find it. And in *our* Trefor's favour, its Wikipedia entry does claim Alice Gray Jones as one of its 'notable people'. So perhaps she was indeed a daughter of Llŷn.

To press on. Alice Gray Jones was a noted temperance campaigner who founded the North Wales Women's Temperance Union. Now I'm not a natural ally of temperance, being fond of the occasional pint, but there was no doubt that the demon drink did cause much distress at that time (as it does today), especially to working-class women. So, an admirable cause.

Alice (though I don't think I'd have dared use such familiarity to her face) was educated at Dolbadarn Primary School (near Llanberis – that place again), became a student teacher at the British Society (ie Non-conformist) School in Caernarfon, trained as a teacher in Swansea, and ended up as head of the Dolbadarn school that she'd attended as a child.

This is where her place of birth becomes irrelevant. Even if she was from exotic, far-away Llanberis, even if her father's family owned a woollen mill there, even if she went to school and eventually became a headteacher in Dolbadarn, from 1881 Llŷn could unquestionably claim her as its own. In that year she married the Reverend William Jones, the vicar of Y Ffôr, and lived there and had with him, appropriately enough, four children.

In 1893 Alice became a governor of Pwllheli's County School, precursor of Ysgol Ramadeg Pwllheli. Which I attended. Why were we pupils not told of this claim to fame? And if we had been, would we have cared?

During the late nineteenth and early twentieth centuries, under her pseudonym, Alice went from strength to strength – as a poet, children's author and journalist. She wrote for Welsh-language *Y Frythones*, *Y Traethodydd*, and *Y Gymraes*, the last of which she also edited. When her husband retired in 1919, the couple moved to Cricieth. Two years later she was awarded an OBE. Though not, I'm sure, just because she moved to Cricieth, lovely though it is.

Alice Gray Jones, Ceridwen Peris, an admirable and formidable woman, died at her daughter's house in Bangor during the Second World War. She was ninety years old.

Postscript

With reference to this first section of writers on the 'Literary Map of Wales', the resulting comments could be classified as geographical, facetious or literary.

1. Geographical discussion centred on how we should define the Llŷn Peninsula. My rule of thumb was that Llŷn is everything west of a line drawn from Porthmadog to Caernarfon, though I confess that on occasion I swung the line eastward from Caernarfon to Bangor, so that I could include more people that I wanted to write about.

2. Facetious comment was kicked off by my brother, who offered the opinion that my wife would probably have been happy to buy me a Ferrari if it wasn't for 'access issues', i.e. the difficulties for old people of managing a low-slung sports car. When I challenged him about what he meant, he insisted that his only thought was of the stiff joints of our father, and the grunts that accompanied any physical effort that he made, both of which I now seem to have inherited. Another group member helpfully

extended the possible interpretations by posting a clip of an obese man struggling to get out of a similarly low-slung car, to a soundtrack of a woman's helplessly hysterical laughter.

3. Far more erudite literary discussion arose from a post about other *Beirdd yr Uchelwyr* studied at 'A' Level. It included mention of Cysur Henaint, with his lament about extreme old age (which I haven't been able to unearth, but with which I sympathise) and a poem by Lewys Glyn Cothi (*c.*1420–1490) about the death of his five-year-old son (Siôn y Glyn). I found a copy online. Written over five hundred years ago, it still breaks your heart. Here's an extract:

Marwnad Siôn y Glyn

Fy mab, fy muarth baban,
fy mron, fy nghalon, fy nghân,
fy mryd cyn fy marw ydoedd,
fy mardd doeth, fy mreuddwyd oedd;
fy nhegan oedd, fy nghannwyll,
fy enaid teg, fy un twyll;
fy nghyw yn dysgu fy nghân,
fy nghae Esyllt, fy nghusan;
fy nyth, gwae fi yn ei ôl,
fy ehedydd, fy hudol;
fy Siôn, fy mwa, fy saeth,
f'ymbiliwr, fy mabolaeth.

At the risk of much hilarity from those who are fluent in Welsh, especially those who may have studied the poem with Beti Jones for 'A' Level, I've tried to translate it. We've all had a giggle at some the 'translate' button's efforts on Facebook, so any help with the meaning would be much appreciated.

Death of Siôn y Glyn

My son, my farmyard baby,
My breast, my heart, my song,
He was the time before my death,
My wise poet, he was my dream;
He was my toy, my candle,
My beautiful soul, my only deceit;
My chick learning/teaching my song,
My Isolde's field, my kiss;
My nest, my woe after him,
My skylark, my enchantment;
My whisper, my bow, my arrow,
My supplicant, my boyhood.

I can't claim to understand it all – the *treigladau* (mutations) make it difficult to look words up in the dictionary – but what I do understand really packs a punch. The pain of a parent who lost a child over five hundred years ago overcoming the barriers of time and language. Hard to read without crying.

Pretty deep stuff, eh? I dread to think what my chum Tony Pierce will make of it! But hey – sometimes you've got to risk being accused of being pretentious. Pretentious? *Moi?*

I'll leave the last word to Brenda Jones who started the whole discussion.

'Who'd have thought that a chance mention would lead to a discussion of fifteenth-century Welsh poetry on this site? Sublime! And I like to think that Beti Jones would be tickled pink!'

Hester Lynch Piozzi

The most impressive, most spectacular, of the names to be plastered across Llŷn on the 'Literary Map of Wales' was Hester Lynch Piozzi. No, I'd never heard of her either.

Her claims to historical significance are undeniable. She was a top-end poshy, only daughter of Sir John Salusbury, a member of 'one of the most illustrious Welsh land-owning dynasties of the Georgian era'. She said of herself that she 'was taught to read and speak and think and translate from the French till I was half a prodigy.' Or, as we'd say today, 'til I was blue in the face'.

Hester Lynch Piozzi was a substantial figure, well-known in polite society, a confidant of Dr Johnson no less. Yet eventually she disgraced herself by marrying an Italian music teacher.

Hester was born in Bodfel Hall. This is just off a road that, as a teenager, I strode along with my mates in the dead of night singing Beatles songs on the way back to Pwllheli after a night at the Sportsman in Nefyn. Though she, of course, wouldn't have been aware of this.

Her first husband was Henry Thrale, a rich brewer, who after their marriage allowed her the freedom to associate with whomsoever she pleased. I'm surprised she had time – they had twelve children. But she moved in elevated circles – apart from Dr Johnson, she met James Boswell, Oliver Goldsmith and other noted literary figures.

After Thrale's death in 1781, she married her children's music teacher – Gabriel Mario Piozzi. This was social death, the equivalent of marrying the help, and a foreigner to boot. She was universally condemned, and retired with her husband to her estate in Denbighshire, there to lick her wounds and consider the error of her ways. Or perhaps not. She called the estate Brynbella, a name which was half Welsh (Bryn) and half Italian (Bella). So I'm guessing that she wasn't all that bothered by the universal disapprobation. The house is just off the A55, apparently – I'll take a look the next time I'm driving past.

Dilys Cadwaladr

A Welsh-language poet and fiction writer, Dilys Cadwaladr (1902–1979) was the first female to win a crown at the

National Eisteddfod. That was in Rhyl, in 1953. Now her Llŷn credentials at first gave me pause – she was born just outside Llanrwst, and however I draw the line dividing Llŷn from the rest of north Wales, I can't get it to include the Conwy valley. But she was interesting. Not only was she a female trailblazer, but she had a 'close relationship' with elderly poet Dewi Emrys (1881–1952). In fact, she bore him a daughter in 1930. They don't get much closer than that. No, her main claim to being a part of Llŷn's literary heritage is that, during the 1940s, she lived on Ynys Enlli, as both a farmer and as schoolteacher to the island's few children.

I'm very much aware of the huge gaps in this account. In the 1940s, for example, when Dilys was living on Bardsey, where was 'elderly poet' Dewi Emrys? And what happened between Llanrhychwyn, 1902, where and when she was born, and living on Bardsey in the 1940s? And between then and her triumph in Rhyl in 1953? Too many gaps. This needs a biographer, not a memoirist.

Postscript

Two of the comments following this post referred to Hester Lynch Piozzi.

1. A member of the group used to walk past Bodfel Hall every day, and felt aggrieved that he'd never been told her story. We really need to address this sort of failure in our educational system.

2. Another member knew Piozzi's house Brynbella, but, knowing nothing of its history, had assumed that both words were Welsh. The Italian origin of the second word was a revelation! To bring things up to date, the current owner has a collection of classic cars, though apparently they're not open to the public. I don't know what to do with that.

Carneddog

Richard Griffith (1861–1947) was a Welsh-language poet, writer and journalist who spent nearly all his life in Eryri. He was born on the family farm, Y Carnedd, in Nantmor, just south of Beddgelert, and continued sheep farming all his life. He wrote for *Baner ac Amserau Cymru* and *Yr Herald Cymraeg*, both publications of which I've actually heard.

In idly surfing the net, two things jumped out at me:

1. A beautiful photograph, taken in 1945 by Geoff Charles, of Richard Griffith and this wife Catrin, against the backdrop of their beloved Eryri mountains. They look old (they were in their eighties) but hugely dignified, and the picture was taken to mark their leaving the farm to live with their son in Hinckley, in the English Midlands.

2. In Googling 'Nantmor', I discovered the following:

- It was the home of Dafydd Nanmor (the old spelling of Nantmor), a fifteenth-century bard.

- It was where *The Inn of the Sixth Happiness*, a feature film about Gladys Aylward, was filmed in the late 1950s. It starred Ingrid Bergman, Robert Donat and Kurt Jurgens.

- It was the scene, too, of a trilogy of books written by Ruth Janette Ruck, about life on her farm ('Carnedd') in the 1950s, '60s and '70s. Perhaps she bought the farm from Richard Griffith?

All well and good. But not a single mention of Richard and Catrin Griffith.

As a child I remember the excitement caused in Pwllheli by the Ingrid Bergman film. Coach trips went to look at the re-creation of a Chinese town up in the mountains. I don't remember *Place of Stones*, *Hill Farm Story*, or *Along Came a Llama*, the books written by Ruth Janette Ruck about her life on the farm. And I certainly have not heard of Dafydd

Nanmor – was everybody a bard in those days? Wales seemed to be knee-deep in them.

But as a man in my late seventies, the image of Richard Griffith, leaving the farm where he was born and in which he'd lived for the whole of his life up until then, surrounded by the spectacular mountain scenery which had sustained him, for presumably more anodyne suburban Hinckley (between Coventry and Leicester) somehow hit home. Not, surprisingly, as an image of defeat and displacement, but of graceful acceptance of the inevitable, of dignified submission to the imperative of the forward impetus of time, and of the next generation's acceptance of its responsibilities to its precursors. Or so, with my children in mind, I fervently hope.

Richard Griffith died two years after the move.

Eben Fardd

Eben Fardd was the bardic name of Ebenezer Thomas (1802–1863), poet and teacher. His Llŷn credentials are impeccable – he was born in Llanarmon, between Chwilog and Y Ffôr, and on his brother William's death, took over as headteacher of his school in Llangybi. Nepotism, as we'd call it today. Eben Fardd won the poetry prize in Liverpool and Welshpool eisteddfods. In 1827 he moved to Clynnog Fawr (into a house called Bod Cybi, opposite the church – must check to see if it's still there). He is mainly remembered today as a hymn writer: his most famous hymn 'O! Fy Iesu bendigedig' ('Oh my blessed Jesus') was written in response to the deaths, in quick succession, of his wife and three of his four children. If his faith survived that, he's a better man than I am.

Eben Fardd died and was buried in the churchyard in Clynnog Fawr – you can't miss his monument.

Postscript

1. There was much sympathy for Richard Griffith as he and his wife left the beauties of Eryri for Hinckley – assumed to be some sort of Midlands living-death. I initially felt the same, though researching Hinckley brought home to me that everywhere has its history and its unique character. Hinckley was a major centre for the hosiery industry, was home to Triumph motorcycles and Una Stubbs, and was the birthplace of Davy Graham, ace folk guitarist who influenced Bert Jansch, John Renbourn, Martin Carthy, John Martyn, Paul Simon and Jimmy Page. Though I have to admit that he didn't seem to have lived there for very long. When I first bought a guitar, all I could manage, after weeks of diligent toil, was a fumblingly approximate version of his 'Angie'. It didn't impress a guitar-shop proprieter in London's Denmark Street, but that's another story. So Hinckley has no need to be modest about its achievements. Though it was, and probably still is, short of mountains.

2. There is a Welsh history centre in Clynnog Fawr called Canolfan Uwchgwyrfai which hosts a reading group called *Cyfeillion Eban*, after Eben Fardd. I'm not sure whether that 'Eban' should be 'Eben', since it's short for Ebenezer. But that's what it's called online.

3. A member of our group heard Gladys Aylward give a talk in a Llŷn chapel in the late 1960s. A comment that so brings the past to life. You never think of famous people like her, portrayed in the '50s on screen by Ingrid Bergman, living through the Swinging Sixties and then, just before her death, sharing memories of her life. In Tudweiliog.

Dic Tryfan

Dic Tryfan (the bardic name for Richard Hughes Williams, 1878–1919) was born in Rhosgadfan, just south-west of Llanberis, and is mainly known for his short stories. He belonged to a quarrying family, and he himself worked in the quarries when young, though made his living as an adult from his writing for Welsh-language newspapers and periodicals.

Dic Tryfan wrote mainly about the physical hardships, poverty and danger of life in the slate quarries, not pulling any punches but also emphasizing the courage, sense of humour and spirit of solidarity shared by the quarrymen. His work was admired, though not without reservation, by our next writer.

Kate Roberts

Kate Roberts (1891–1985) was another product of the village of Rhosgadfan (population half that of Pwllheli – there must have been something in the water) and was one of the giants of twentieth-century Welsh-language writing. She too was the child of a quarryman. Her novels, short-stories and autobiography give a vivid picture of life in and around Bethesda.

Born in Denbigh, she was brought up in the family cottage of Cae'r Gors, graduated at Bangor University, and became a teacher, taking up positions in Dolbadarn, Ystralyfera and Aberdare. She met her husband, Morris T Williams, through Plaid Cymru, and after they married in 1928 the couple bought a printing press, Gwasg Gee, and published books, pamphlets and *Y Faner*, a weekly Welsh-language newspaper. She continued publishing for ten years after his death in 1946.

In 1965 Kate Roberts bought her childhood home Cae'r Gors and presented it to the nation. It eventually, when the necessary money could be scraped together, opened as a museum devoted to her life and work.

Three factoids about Kate Roberts:

- She became a writer after the death of her brother during the First World War.

- She had a forty-year friendship with controversial national figure, Saunders Lewis.

- She was at the centre of rumours about her sexuality (sparked by her admission, in a letter to her husband, that kissing a woman had made her supremely happy).

Another admirable figure, though I can't help feeling that buying Cae'r Gors for the nation was a bit presumptuous.

Eifion Wyn

Eliseus Williams (what were his parents thinking?), bardic name Eifion Wyn (1867–1926), was born and bred in Porthmadog, where he spent thirty years of his life as clerk and accountant to the North Wales Slate Company.

- He was a prolific poet and writer, with many eisteddfod prizes and a book of hymns for children to his name.

- His wife Ann Jones was from Abererch.

- His hobbies included fishing and billiards. It had never occurred to me that poets might have hobbies – a real failure of imagination on my part. OK, I find it easy to picture this noted Welsh bard sitting on the banks of Afon Glaslyn, the mountains of Eryri in the distance and a far-away look in his eye, jotting down an idea for an *englyn* while the bobbing of his float goes unnoticed. But potting balls and lining up canons in a smoky billiard-hall, perhaps with a cigarette hanging from his lower lip? Not so much. Yet I find it somehow comforting. As I said, a failure of my imagination.

Eifion Wyn is buried in Chwilog.

216

Cynan

I've left Cynan (Albert Evans-Jones, 1895–1970) till last, not only because he was one of the most important figures in Welsh literature and in the development of the Eisteddfod movement, but because he was born in my home town (Pwllheli) and went to the same school (Ysgol Ramadeg Pwllheli) as I did. I think we studied several of his poems at 'O' Level, though I'm sure those taking 'hard Welsh' will have read a lot more and will have found out far more about him. Cynan's father owned the Central Restaurant, at the top of Penlan Street, opposite the Town Hall. I remember, as a child, reading the plaque mounted on the outside wall of the building as I entered the public library to get books for my parents.

Cynan was the only National Eisteddford archdruid to be elected twice. He drove the modernisation of its rules and procedures, and was responsible for accepting that a lot of the eighteenth-century claims of Iolo Morganwg – that the Eisteddfod went back to ancient Welsh mythology and druidical traditions – was a load of old tosh. He introduced a host of new ceremonies which were more in line with Christian tradition (he was after all a Presbyterian minister), but which were also a lot of fun. I can't help feeling that, as he sat designing them, there was a twinkle in his eye and a tongue in his cheek.

But lest we forget. Cynan was a wonderful poet. I know several of his poems (though I'm not going to say which ones, in case they're by somebody else). He is widely considered to be a finer war poet than Hedd Wyn (who, incidentally, only failed to make the cut for this post by the thinnest of margins – he was from Trawsfynydd). And I felt that Hedd Wyn has already received more than his fair share of adulation – a host of literary and musical mentions, and an Oscar-nominated film, no less.

Finally, I really envy Cynan's place of burial – on Church Island, in the Menai Straits. I wouldn't mind being buried there myself. Though not yet.

Take a peek at the photographs of Cynan online. He looks really jolly, really relatable. Which is not always true of earlier writers from the north-west of Wales.

Postscript

Comments included two choice bits of gossip which, curiously, made their subjects, both giants of Llŷn literature, more human:

1. A teacher at Glan-y-Môr shared with one of his pupils that, as a boy, he lived next door to Kate Roberts. 'Better not let your ball go into her garden,' he said, 'or you'd never get it back.'

2. Cynan, it was rumoured with a nod, a wink and a nudge, was a bit of a ladies' man. And him a minister! I'm not going to go there – I don't want to be sued. I came across his biography by Gerwyn Williams in Llandudno Waterstones, and discovered that his grandparents lived in Llŷn Street, just up the road from where I was born and bred! I didn't buy the book – it's huge, and in Welsh. Perhaps when I've honed my Welsh-language skills? Or when they bring out a translation? Or when hell freezes over – I'm already well past my threescore years and ten, and I need to prioritise before the coming dark. The dark that lights no lamps.

Conclusion

As may be clear from the above account, I hit two major problems in my research:

Names

In Wales, for no doubt perfectly valid historical reasons, we Welsh seem to share a very limited range of surnames. This can create considerable confusion when doing the sort of superficial fact-scan to which I'm prone. Consider – the

surnames of the main heroes of my research were:
- Jones
- Griffith
- Williams
- Roberts
- Williams again
- Evans-Jones

If I wasn't myself Welsh, I might think that they were taking the piss.

The Welsh language

My Welsh is poor. For this I've nobody to blame but myself. In writing about and judging poetry, novels and short stories written in the Welsh language, this is something of a disadvantage, if not a fatal flaw. I can't read Welsh literature in the original, and so must rely on the opinions of others. Or Google translate. And that, I think we've already established, can be very hit and miss.

When I started investigating the literary heritage of the Llŷn Peninsula, I at first thought that these two problems would crash the project before it got off the ground. But two factors came to the rescue:

Bardic names

Bardic names were names awarded to poets, by themselves or others, no doubt to help in distinguishing one bard from another who had the same surname. Without bardic names, any study of Welsh literature would become a nightmare. Imagine the chair or crown being awarded to the wrong Jones, or Williams, or Roberts. The same function is served by nicknames – from my own childhood, some that spring to mind are John Isallt, Williams 80, Will Cap Coch, Bob Workhouse and Mary Sîop Chips. Or even my own father, Mr Simon Penlleiniau.

Welsh culture

As I read about the writers who created the literature of
north-west Wales, what emerged was a tapestry of farm-
labourers, shepherds, slate-quarrymen, teachers, preachers
and journalists, of Non-conformist chapels, *cymanfaoedd canu*
and eisteddfodau, all in the Welsh language, which provided
the rich soil from which this literature grew. Not only that,
but it created a 'canon' of accepted judgements which I could
use – if you lack the knowledge yourself, then make sure the
judgements of others that you use are informed and well-
founded.

In future I may consult the 'Literary Map of Wales' again,
looking for writers associated with other places I know – the
Rhondda Valley, for example, where my parents grew up, or
the area around Conwy, Bae Colwyn and Llandudno, which
has become my second home. But for the time being I'll let the
writers of the past rest in peace.

CHAPTER 20

Travel writers on Wales

READING TRAVEL BOOKS about Wales and the Welsh gave me an interesting outside view of our country. I've already written about George Borrow, but several others are worth a mention:

1. Pamela Petro

As a late convert to both reading and writing about travel, and a recent reconnector with my Llŷn heritage, I could only envy Pamela Petro's inspired idea of linking her fascination with all things Welsh with a general interest in travel and a particular interest in *hiraeth*.

She's a highly reckoned American writer who, for no discernible reason, decided to learn Welsh, which she did by signing up for courses at Lampeter. Finding that most Welsh-speakers in Wales spoke English, and therefore courteously switched language when all she wanted to do was practise her Welsh, she decided to visit Welsh-speaking communities all over the world, something a book proposal with resulting advance and a series of articles allowed her to finance. Her account, in *Travels in an Old Tongue*, is not only very engaging and very funny, but it's format – starting each anecdote with a Welsh word – reminded me of many I'd forgotten and introduced me to a few I never knew. That said, by and large, she found that Welsh communities abroad also tended courteously to switch to English when they felt that that the person they were speaking to, however well motivated, was struggling. A lovely book, with characters we would all recognise in our own communities.

2. H V Morton

A mate of mine a few years back, knowing that I was doing some travel writing and that I was Welsh, gave me a copy of *In Search of Wales* by H V Morton. Reading the book, then doing some research, threw up a fascinating story.

Morton was an English journalist, star reporter for the *Daily Express* and then the *Daily Herald* in the 1920s and '30s. While covering all the various news items that being a staffer on national newspapers involved (including the opening of the tomb of Tutankhamun), he also started to write travel pieces, initially about London, then arising from motoring tours of Britain, and progressing to tours of the Holy Land. Not only did he find that he enjoyed researching and writing these travel articles more than the grunt work of a professional journalist, he was also delighted that, when they were compiled into a series of books, starting with *In Search of England*, they were hugely popular, sold in their thousands, and made him very rich.

I open my rather handsome Minerva edition of *In Search of Wales* (faux-leather covers, map of his route). It begins, 'Twenty years ago I set out for Wales. I was in love with a girl who was spending a holiday with her family in Pwllheli.' Her family weren't, alas, as impressed with him as she was. They greeted him coldly and sent him on his way. He spent a weekend in a lowly cottage room in Llanbedrog, from which he was, in due course, ejected in favour of a family who'd booked the room from the Monday. With his tail between his legs, he returned to Pwllheli to fall upon the charity of his beloved's family. Again to no avail. The weekend did nothing to improve his chances. He was nineteen. You've got to feel for him.

This memory sparks off, twenty years later, a tour of the Principality. Now pushing forty, a bit of a celebrity and looking to add to his *In search of...* travel books, he enters Wales in his little two-seater roadster across the bridge at Chirk, then later leaves Wales via Monmouth. In between he drives all over the country, describing what he sees, stitching in bits of history, relating conversations he had with the people along the way, telling stories which are often very funny. A bit like George Borrow (whose book he must have read and, to an extent, based his own book on). But this was eighty years later, and he was much more urbane, much less pompous, and with a fine Roaring Twenties sense of humour.

His emphasis is certainly on north Wales – eight chapters are about the north, two each about mid and south Wales. I don't want to end up rewriting the whole book, so I'll concentrate on the bits of north Wales that I know.

I'll join the author in a pub in Rhuddlan, between Rhyl and St Asaph.

He meets a disgruntled 'superior person' who is a keen fisherman. He is, it turns out, disgruntled partly because he has lost his very expensive rod (it fell off the running board of his sports car – don't you hate it when that happens?), and partly because, wherever he's fished with his top-of-the-range gear and his sophisticated flies, he's been outdone by local lads using the equivalent of a branch cut from the hedge, a length of line, and a maggot. Shades (for those who remember it) of Elvis Presley in *Follow That Dream*!

From Rhuddlan he takes in Rhyl ('I like windy Rhyl') and then 'one of the most fascinating and beautiful highways in Great Britain... a corniche road serving a kind of Welsh Riviera.' That's from Rhyl to Caernarfon, long before they built the North Wales Expressway. He extols the 'quiet little places like Abergele' with 'its woody hills at the back'. He even mentions Llanddulas, where 'poor Richard II was betrayed into the hands of Bolingbroke.' And where incidentally, though in the scheme of things not quite so important and as mentioned earlier, my wife and I bought a static caravan. Not that that would have been much consolation to Richard II, who died (apparently) of starvation in Pontefract. Where, oddly, my wife once worked. Not in the castle where he died, but in a local authority school. And again, that wouldn't have been much consolation to Richard II. But it's these personal little details that fix places in your memory.

To return to Henry Morton. He arrives in Colwyn Bay and admires its 'gold sands, a great half circle of sea, hills, woods and streams', finding that its 'charm and popularity' is 'due to the fact that you can be tucked away in the town, but half an hour's walking takes you to hills and winds from the Atlantic'.

As he does throughout the book, he alternates his own impressions and experiences with bits of local history and folklore – in this case, the story of the Cursing Well of Llanelian-yn-Rhos, a village in the hills behind the town. The gullible, he explains, believed that you could curse somebody (your rival in love, say, or a business competitor) simply by paying the well-keeper a fee, who would gratefully accept the cash and, with suitable mumbo-jumbo, impose the curse. Then later, if requested by the quaking object of the spell and with equally suitable reverse mumbo-jumbo, accept a similar amount of money and remove the curse. A nice little earner!

Henry (you see how he and I have now become friends) likes Llandudno, though he has no delusions about it ('It knows its job. It knows exactly what people want'). He absolutely loves Conwy, extolling it above far more famous walled towns like Chester and York. He admires Telford's suspension bridge ('It has been made to blend in with Conway Castle. It even forms a perfect approach to it. It is one of the best examples I know of good manners in architecture.') In my opinion, ninety years later, driving across the new road bridge, built long after he visited, is just as perfect an approach to this most perfect of towns.

Having left Conwy via the Sychnant Pass, and bowling along in his open-topped sports car, he notices the voices of children singing in a school he's passing. Ever the hotshot reporter, he stops, enters it and talks to the headteacher. 'They've been practising for the coming National Eisteddfod', the head tells him, 'in Bangor.' Since the choristers have now dispersed, Henry asks if he might return when next they rehearse. The head will have none of it, and rushes off to fetch the music master (inevitably a Mr Jones) who assembles the girls from their classrooms. Morton is introduced as a great musician who has come all the way from London just to hear them sing (we Welsh, they say, never let the truth interfere with a good story). Henry describes the teenage girls: 'These long-legged, inky-fingered, spotty or peach-faced, funny little fawn-like creatures' who, he conjectures, 'in another eight years would be the wives and mothers of Wales. It was rather terrifying, like watching the manufacture of explosives.'

This is followed by a detailed account of his impressions of Bangor ('one of the freshest and most stimulating cities you can imagine'). In his hotel he is captivated by the sound of a young woman practising on the harp, preparing, her husband tells him, for the Eisteddfod. And in his visit to the Eisteddfod field itself, he observes the ceremonials ('I am slightly worried by the trousers of bard and druid which are visible for a few inches below their gowns. Father Christmas has this same trouble.'). He chats with a young man on the Maes, who, shortly afterwards, is dragged forward in the pavilion (looking as if 'two burly British policemen were arresting a drunk') and awarded the crown for poetry. Yes indeed, this was Cynan, from Pwllheli.

Another young man, in plus-fours, makes an appearance, reverently placing a wreath of leaves, to which he seemed to be talking, before the high altar. He was, it turns out, conversing via its concealed microphone to colleagues in the distant wireless van. He worked for the infant BBC, which was preparing to broadcast the proceedings.

Elsewhere in his account of the Eisteddfod, he quotes in full a poem by Lewys Glyn Cothi, who'd performed at a wedding in Fflint, had received a poor reception from guests who much preferred the contribution of a piper called William Beisir, and made his displeasure known in no uncertain terms. The poem is a ferocious, and very funny, attack on bagpipes in general, and Beisir in particular – 'And I midst laughter was dismissed, for William Beisir's bag they bawl.' A far cry from the heart-rending lament for his dead five-year-old son (see page 208).

After a diversion into Môn (Beaumaris, Llangefni, and an aside about the origins of the Tudors), Morton arrives in Caernarfon. He's impressed by the castle (who wouldn't be?) then progresses towards Llŷn.

In Clynnog Fawr he is much taken (as was I when I visited it more recently) by the expanding tongs, used to expel unruly dogs while keeping them at a safe arm's length. This reminds him of a story where a vicar's dog (called 'Tango') got into such a ferocious fight with a visiting farmer's dog that the service had to be abandoned. 'Above the roar and snarl of battle,' he explains, the congregation heard their vicar bellow, 'Three to one on Tango'.

From Pwllheli ('a very ordinary little sea-side town,' he scoffs, perhaps reminded of his humiliation twenty years before) he heads for Aberdaron, stopping at Sarn for a pint. What strikes him is the contrast between the remoteness and backwardness that guidebooks led him to expect as he travelled west along the Llŷn Peninsula, and the many signs of modern life he encountered:

- In the Sarn pub the barman is reading an English newspaper, published in Liverpool the night before.
- And in Aberdaron:
  o Many of the houses sport radio aerials.

o The Barclays Bank opens for business in a cottage front room every Monday.

o And in the local hostelry (not the village inn he expected, but a 'good little hotel') he encounters two young men in golf clothes sipping 'gins and It' at a 'perfectly sophisticated bar'. Morton continues, 'This was Aberdaron, the place in which I expected to see ancient Britons clothed in skins!'

• Henry tries to visit Ynys Enlli, but the Aberdaron boatmen refuse to take him, saying that although they could probably get him onto the island, he might be marooned there for days because a storm was brewing.

He heads back to Pwllheli and on to Cricieth. He can't drag his eyes away from the view. 'I have never seen anything more magnificent than the incredible panorama of sea and mountains that faces Cricieth across ten or fifteen miles of blue-green water.' Anybody who's visited Cricieth will know exactly what he means.

Being in Cricieth, Henry is reminded of its most famous resident, Lloyd George. 'The Welsh Wizard,' he says, 'is one of the greatest personalities of our time,' who 'took charge of the destinies of the British Empire during the darkest moment in our history.' This was, of course, eight years before the outbreak of the Second World War, when even darker moments loomed.

Lloyd George was clearly something of a hero to Morton. He goes on to outline the event which first made him (Lloyd George) a national figure – the 'Llanfrothen burial case'. A Non-conformist quarryman on his deathbed expressed a wish to be buried in the churchyard near the grave of his child. But, because the quarryman was chapel, it was thought unlikely that this request would be granted. Lloyd George, the local solicitor, encouraged people, if the request were to be denied, to break down the churchyard wall. The vicar duly refused, and the people duly broke down the wall. They were fined for their trouble, but Lloyd George appealed on their behalf, and the fines were quashed. This earned him not only widespread acclaim in Wales, but a nomination as the Liberal Parliamentary candidate for the constituency of Caernarfon Boroughs.

Morton sets off for Llanystumdwy to take a look at Lloyd George's birthplace. On the way back to Cricieth, near Bryn Awelon, Lloyd George's house on the northern edge of the town, he encounters a man in a brown suit. 'His picturesque silver hair was visible under a tweed hat, and his blue eyes looked keenly at the world from a nest of good-humoured wrinkles.' Yes indeed – it was Lloyd George himself! They talk extensively about the Welsh landscape, Welsh history, the Welsh Non-conformist revival, and the Welsh language. Their conversation ends with Lloyd George telling the story of a great preacher – John Elias – who visited a chapel the night before he was due to preach there. He lit candles in various parts of the auditorium, then, standing in the pulpit, instructed the caretaker to extinguish selected ones. These he got rid of, then blew out the remaining candles, and left them in place ready to be lit at the start of the service the next day. During his sermon 'he worked up his audience to a pitch of fervour and then, as he spoke about the Finger of the Lord, flung out a hand. The congregation saw, with something like terror, an enormous shadowy finger printed by the light of the candles on the walls of the chapel.'

Having followed Morton's route through the parts of north Wales that I know, I left him to continue on his eccentric way, through Beddgelert, Llanberis, Snowdon, Harlech, Dolgellau, Bala, Aberystwyth, Machynlleth, Rhyader, Llandrindod Wells, Cardigan, Fishguard, St Davids, Carmarthen, and on to the heavy industry of Llanelli, Swansea, Cardiff and the Rhondda Valleys. In addition to describing the places he visits, he supplies character sketches of the people he meets, and entertainingly holds forth on numerous subjects that occur to him along the way – sheepdogs, Welsh Sundays, King Arthur, war memorials, the manufacture of tweed, Welsh rain, coracles, steel working, copper smelting, donkey racing among the cockle women of the Gower, and male voice choirs. And many, many more. His account of a trip down a coal mine, and his observations about the hard lives and rich culture of the miners, are arresting and very sympathetic.

To sum up. It's hard to dislike H V Morton when you read his book. He's urbane, observant, funny, writes well, and completely avoids that patronising attitude to us Welsh that you can find among some other visitors to our country. But there are downsides. Though there are no traces of it in the book, he was extremely right wing, a womaniser, a racist and an antisemite. He eventually emigrated to South Africa where he saw out his days. A place more sympathetic to his views, presumably. Hard to square this with his affecting account of the miners and steelworkers of south Wales, or his sympathetic treatment of all things Welsh in his lovely book.

I'll conclude with the words of one of my all-time favourites – Jan Morris.

She said of H V Morton that he was, 'A much-loved master of his genre, often imitated but never matched. His books are genuine classics.' So who better to end this section than Jan Morris?

3. Jan Morris

Jan Morris, a much-loved Llŷn celebrity, was an idol to me in so many ways. She:

- Chose to live in Llanystymdwy for over half a century, even though she:
  o must have been almost everywhere in the world;
  o was worth a bob or two and
  o could have lived wherever the hell she liked.
- Identified strongly with the Welsh side of her Anglo-Welsh parentage.

- Occupied a converted chapel lined with thousands of books. I'm green with envy.

- Was, like me, an inveterate and annoying whistler.

- Was the first to report on the conquest of Everest in 1953. After all, David and Steven Morgan and I attended Pwllheli carnival that year as Hunt, Hillary and Tenzing. What a connection!

- Was born a man and became a woman. I have a grandchild who was born a girl, declared herself a boy, and now – who knows. And another who's making up their mind. Not 'her' mind – she doesn't wish to be categorised. And they do have a point. They are thirteen.

- Wrote not only wonderful travel books (her *Venice* dragged my wife and me away from the tourist haunts, at least for an afternoon), but also a range of excellent pieces including one about her attitude to Wales, and another putting forward her vision of its future:

  o In the one she explains why she chose to be Welsh. Although always aware of being half Welsh (her father was from Monmouthshire), she had written many times about Wales as an outsider. Then, in the 1960s, she received a letter from J E Jones, a gardener and Plaid leader, suggesting that she should 'embrace it [Welshness] in its fullness and make [herself] a true part of it.' It was an epiphany. It changed her whole attitude to Wales, and she never looked back.

  o In the other she puts forward her vision of an independent Wales. She conjures up a vision of a small republic, proud in its independence but, in foreign affairs, 'formally neutral' but 'an enthusiastic member of the EU'. She does describe its capital, Machynlleth, as a sea-coast town (eh?), though this might be part of the light-hearted wish that this new country would be perfect in every way. It would have no taxation, for example, and a climate approximating that of Bermuda.

Furthermore:

- Her advice about travel-writing (especially that, 'If somebody chances to pick my pocket or be rude to me on a bus... it is not because he's German, or American, or Arab, or Indian, or English, but because he is a thief or a yob, just like the ones we have in Wales.') changed my attitude to travel. Her writing was brave, self-deprecating, amused and above all informed.

- Her brother, despite all her achievements, still couldn't get himself to use the pronoun 'her' when talking about his sibling. I find it comforting when faced with similar difficulties when dealing with my grandchildren, though I hope I'm making a better fist of it.

- She married wife Elizabeth in 1949. They stayed together during his transition and gender reassignment in the 1960s and 1970s, and as soon as it was legal, entered a civil partnership (in Pwllheli, I seem to remember). They had five children, one of whom is prominent Welsh poet and musician Twm Morys.

- Jan Morris died in Bryn Beryl. As did my mother.

CHAPTER 21

Stop press!

Completing the circle

My six months' initial deep dive into Welsh culture ended
when we finally moved back from Llanddulas into our new
house in north Staffordshire. This was at the beginning of
September 2023. Fetching furniture out of storage, organising
its installation, sorting out internet connection, redecorating
throughout, building a new patio, all this left little time for
memoir-writing.

Menter y Tŵr

But while dodging decorators and builders (no, we didn't do it
ourselves – we're getting on for eighty, for heaven's sake!) and
trying to get ready for the family Christmas invasion, I noticed
that Pwllheli was raising money to buy the semi-derelict Tower
Hotel (Y Tŵr) in the centre of the town, with a view to developing
it as a community resource. So as Christmas presents, I bought
shares for my brother and myself, to maintain our link with
what we still think of as home.

The Tower – an imposing building centrally placed on the
High Street – seemed to have echoed through my memories of
growing up in Pwllheli:

- When I was a little kid I used to watch Pwllheli and District play in the Welsh League Division North, and I was very much aware that the jewel in our crown was Tommy Jones, ex-Everton and England professional, now proprietor of Y Twr, and player-manager of the team.

- When my cousin Jill got married, my father gave an excellent speech at the reception in the Tower. He was standing in for Uncle Dick, who couldn't make it up from south Wales.

- My younger brother tells me that he had his first legal drink in the Tower's cocktail bar. Could be worth a blue plaque!

- I used to frequent the same cocktail bar (on the first floor) during trips back home.

- During my many years as a choirboy at St Peter's Church, I and my co-choristers would duck into the Tower's back yard for a quick cigarette before the services started.

- We also used to shin up the telegraph pole cable in Church Street, next to the hotel, giving us access to the roofs of the rear yard buildings. Why we'd want such access I've no idea.

- I can't say that in later years I used the bar in the Tower an awful lot. On visits back to Pwllheli I tended to use the Castle, the Whitehall, the Mitre and the Penlan Fawr. But I did sometimes pop in for a pint, usually with Robert Roberts, who'd taken over as St Peter's organist after Dad died.

Although I can't claim a huge connection to the Tower then, I certainly feel growing excitement at the prospect of its proposed community redevelopment. What a great idea, and a tribute to all those who've given up their time to do the huge amount of work it entails.

Capel Salem

Not long after the drive to renovate Y Tŵr as a community project got under way, the news broke that TV celebrity potter Keith Brymer-Jones and his wife intended rescuing the increasingly derelict Capel Salem, with plans to install a studio and living quarters, and eventually open it up to the community. The TV series following this process made celebrities not only of the chapel and the town, but of a number of local residents. Including Marel, my friend Dei Bach's sister.

If Y Tŵr played little part in my growing up, Capel Salem played even less. My father was the organist and choirmaster of St Peter's Church, fifty yards along the road from Salem, and I was a (somewhat reluctant) choirboy throughout my childhood. So I never even entered Capel Salem. Ever! But I didn't have to be a committed Methodist to regret its rapid decline after it was closed, to see its broken windows and weeds sprouting all over its façade. At the time of writing, the TV series seems to have ended with the couple living in a container in the chapel car park. I'm assuming that there'll be a second series showing the actual renovation of the chapel.

So thanks to the efforts of those developing Y Tŵr and Capel Salem, Pwllheli seems to be flourishing into the vibrant cultural hub for the whole of Llŷn that God intended it to be.

Yey!

234

Part Six

Conclusions

So, after getting on for five hundred pages spread across two books of memoirs, what conclusions can I draw from all these stories of growing up in Pwllheli sixty years ago, of missing Wales during my subsequent exile, of recent attempts to reconnect before the coming dark?

Hiraeth in general

If you're thinking about Wales, and exile from Wales, you can't avoid the word *hiraeth*. I have to say that, until about four years ago, I thought, when I thought about it at all, that I was impervious to hiraeth. Bit of a hard case, like. But I was wrong. It's a sneaky little bugger is *hiraeth*, which worms its way into your psyche when you're not looking, and least expect it.

I finally left home, after the four-year half-way house of college, in 1968, at the age of twenty-one, never to live in Wales again. I taught in Suffolk, Staffordshire, Derbyshire and Lincolnshire, and during that time *hiraeth* and I were not even on nodding terms. I got married and had kids. As a family we returned to Pwllheli often, though the visits tailed off as relatives and friends died or moved away. After my mother's death, the visits became even more infrequent.

That's that, I thought! I was more likely to ask that my ashes be sprinkled on the pitch at Ipswich Town's Portman Road, or my remains interred in Newcastle-under-Lyme cemetery where my granddaughter promised to drop in for a chat, than leave this world up the chimney of Bangor crematorium, or passing through the gates of Denio cemetery high above Pwllheli, arm-in-arm with Ginge, bearing a carrier-bag full of bottles and singing Beatles songs at the top of our voices.

Then, much to my surprise, while writing posts for a Pwllheli-based Facebook group, *hiraeth* stirred, growled, bared its fangs, and bit me on the bum.

That's how it started.

So what is *hiraeth*, I asked myself. Why not, I thought, deal with it in the form of a Socratic dialogue, of questions and answers? Surely that's what any self-respecting pretentious prat would do? And after all my wife *is* Greek, though not at all ancient.

So here goes:

1. What's the difference between *hiraeth* and *homesickness*?

OK, we'll start with a hard one. I rummaged around on the internet and found a few definitions that might help. The best was that '*hiraeth* is a pull on the heart that conveys a distinct feeling of missing something irretrievably lost'. This from a young writer, Lily Crossley-Baxter, who's from Porthmadog, but lives and works in Japan. So she should know. My own view is that homesickness is more immediate, but more transitory, than *hiraeth*. Homesickness soon passes; *hiraeth* doesn't.

2. What's the difference between *hiraeth* and *nostalgia?*

Another stinker. Nostalgia is perhaps *hiraeth*'s gentler, more other-worldly sister, wafting about ethereally, trailing her fingers in the river like Ophelia but then, instead of dying, springing up, briskly drying off and getting on with life. If homesickness hits you as soon as you move away, nostalgia floats in and out for the rest of your life.

3. OK, so we know what *hiraeth* isn't. So...?

My take on *hiraeth* is that it's a cocktail of homesickness and nostalgia, interlaced with a ferocious longing for the past, for:

- A particular place
- A particular time
- Particular people

And to emphasise again. That's place, time and people *in the past*. People who rattle on about somewhere that you've never visited, a time that you don't remember, or people that you've never met, can be really, really irritating. Obviously.

4. Is *hiraeth* confined to exiles?

Surely, the further away from Wales you live, and the longer you've been away, the stronger must be the *hiraeth*. One member of our group, for example, moved away to Ireland with her husband (also from Pwllheli) and, for fifty years, suffered agonies of *hiraeth*. But on returning to Pwllheli, the *hiraeth* faded, though whether it disappeared entirely or not I can't say. This perhaps is the time to return to the definition of *hiraeth* – the sense of something 'irretrievably lost'.

5. So why can't you just return to the place where you grew up and show *hiraeth* the door?

To state the obvious:

- The place will have changed. And when it does, old fogeys like us will be at the forefront of those shaking our walking sticks and saying that everything was better in the old days.
- The times won't be the same – the world will have moved on.
- The people? They too will have moved on, or will have grown old, or will be dead.

So even if you return, even if you have never left, the place, the time, the people will still be irretrievably lost. You can't outwit *hiraeth* by staying where you were born.

6. Is *hiraeth* confined to the Welsh?

Surely not. Take the Irish. Millions of them emigrated to the USA during the potato famine and their roots still powerfully affect American politics. On St Patrick's day, Chicago's river is dyed green, and American presidents delight in emphasising any Irish links in their lineage that they can rustle up. And take every other minority group in the United States, who clustered together in its big cities, or settled in its wide open spaces, who sustained their emotional links with their homelands through their food, their customs, their beliefs, their language. Surely *they* experienced *hiraeth*? And who can doubt that the boatloads of migrants who land in the UK and are treated with fear, disdain and hatred, who can doubt that they feel *hiraeth* for homelands made uninhabitable through no fault of their own, by war or famine? And I have seen whatever the Greek for *hiraeth* is among my wife's Cypriot family – the food, the music, the culture, the language, the frequent visits home, the engagement with Greek and Cypriot politics.

In short, *hiraeth*, whatever you call it, is common to us all. It's a part of what makes us human.

7. Is *hiraeth* a pleasure or a pain?

Something in between, surely. To be enjoyed but also endured. Like life, or retirement. Or when you were a child, fiddling with a baby tooth just before it came out.

Hiraeth in particular: my *hiraeth*

So much for *hiraeth* in general. What about *hiraeth* in particular? What about my *hiraeth*? A single day this summer summed up the two sides of my relationship with Wales:

- In my dotage after fifty-five years' exile in England, I was able to visit the recent National Eisteddfod in Boduan, just outside Pwllheli, the town of my birth. I regularly attend National Eisteddfods – my last was in Pwllheli in 1955. I was eight. This visit, at seventy-six, was in 2023. So by my reckoning, I'll be due another visit in 2091, give or take, when I'll be one hundred and forty-four. If, as my mother used to say, I'm spared.

I was hugely impressed by the 2023 National Eisteddfod. I'd wondered if the location might have been a problem. Out towards the tip of the Llŷn Peninsula, Boduan isn't the most accessible place in the world. Might this not have reduced attendance? Not a bit of it. Packed car parks surrounding the Maes. Excellent organisation. Loads of stalls and activities, and everyone – I mean everyone – speaking Welsh. Not a word of English did I hear. I expected a watered-down tourist jamboree. Instead I got an unashamed and full-blooded celebration of Welsh culture.

After a quick tour – well hardly quick, the site was enormous – I searched out the two stands where my book (*On Bonfires, Butlins and Being Welsh*, available in all good bookshops and on Amazon in case you'd forgotten) was likely to be on display.

I'm not proud of this venal approach, but many far better writers than I have admitted to doing similar things:

- o Five copies were reasonably visible in the Literature Wales tent – very pleasing.
- o The two in my publisher's tent were slightly disappointing, though they *were* face rather than spine out. I'd hoped for a more prominent display, since the book is about growing up in Pwllheli, just down the road. But then I *am* the author, and I *would* think that. Parents always look out for their offspring.
- o I noticed in passing that somebody had put a book in front of mine in the display. Almost certainly its author. After a shifty look round, I put the interloper somewhere less visible. Indeed, if I'd known who its author was, and if he was smaller than me, I'd have shoved it where the sun doesn't shine. And yes, I know it should be 'smaller than I', not 'me'. I am a writer, after all.

- Returning through Pwllheli's heavy traffic (it was Wednesday, market day), everywhere we passed sparked teenage memories:
  - o Efailnewydd (where Dick Tudweiliog's VW Beetle flipped onto its roof when we were driving back to Pwllheli from a dance).
  - o Bodegroes (posh restaurant now, but to us kids the location of the best conker tree for miles).
  - o Ala Road (where we viewed our friend Ginge's body at his parent's house, where we cut bamboos for bows and arrows in the vicarage garden, where we smoked and played records above Dafydd Bodlew's dad's vet's surgery, where I reported my bike stolen at the police station, then remembered that I'd left it outside the Liberal Club).
  - o To avoid the traffic, my local knowledge took us up Gaol Street (memories of West End Stores, source

of the paraffin that heated our house in Llŷn Street, and Kampala where I swapped my ration coupons for sweets) and around past St Peter's Church (three boring services every Sunday, *Cymru'r Groes* youth club in the church hall) via Sand Street (Ginge's old house and Allt Bartu).

o   Finally, to beautiful Cricieth, flooded with flashbacks of underage drinking and dances, later visits with children and then grandchildren, and those magnificent views across Cardigan Bay to Harlech and Cader Idris.

On this one day, then, two experiences that summed up my relationship with Wales, though in reverse order:

•   From the present: The eisteddfod in Boduan brought home the late flowering of my interest in my background. Celebrating all things Welsh. Surrounded by the Welsh language. Steeped in Welsh history, culture, music.

•   Into the past: The drive from Boduan to Cricieth stirred up memories of my childhood and youth. All done. All fixed. No way of adding to them. When you're old, you've got a lot to look back on, very little to look forward to. And then you die.

This is probably true of us all. The brackets of our lives – the thoughtlessness of youth, when you think you'll live for ever, the *hiraeth* of age, when you realise that you won't. And, in between, just trying to get by, working at life the best way we can. Too busy to wonder whether we were happy or not. Could that be the happiest time of all?

Acknowledgements

Heartfelt thanks again to all who have contributed:

At Y Lolfa:
- To Lefi Gruffudd for agreeing to publish it, sight unseen.
- To Eirian Jones, not only for detailed and sympathetic editing, but also for advice and encouragement, and wrestling with my mangled Welsh.
- To Garmon Gruffudd and Ellyw Jenkins for sound guidance on all aspects of marketing.
- To Alan Thomas, who turned my pretty inferior photographs, taken mainly on my phone, into an impressive display.

At the Ysgolion Pwllheli and District Schools Facebook group:
- To 'she who must be obeyed' Janet Kaiser, the founder and administrator of the group, again for her encyclopaedic knowledge of this part of north Wales, and for her continued support, encouragement and friendship.
- To all those at YPDS who chipped in with a deluge of brilliant posts. At the end of *On Bonfires, Butlins and Being Welsh* I offered generalised thanks to all those who had contributed 'stories, anecdotes, memories, jokes and insights' but didn't name names, on the grounds that there just wasn't room. Re-reading the book after publication brought home to me just how important those contributions were in recreating life in Pwllheli in the 1950s and '60s. So in this second volume, which carries the story up to the present day, I feel that I

really do have to name names – without those contributions the book would have been thin gruel indeed! Reading back over the posts and postscripts, some names came up time and time again, with anecdotes, opinions and memories which were interesting, which widened the picture of the times, and which were often very, very funny.

So, in alphabetical order of surnames, huge thanks to:

Bolton, Garry	Pierce, Tony
Hamilton, Awen	Pritchard, Pauline
Hankin, Janet	Shaw, Paul
Jones, Brenda	Simon, Chris
Jones, Dafyn	Vowell, Tony
Jones, Gareth	

Thanks also to those whose contributions might have been a little less frequent, but were just as relevant and often just as funny:

Beauceron, Sonny	Myerscough, Richard
Broadbent, Davida Owen	Owen, Gwyneth
Corbett, April	Pwllheli Grammar School
Evans, Gwynfor	Roberts, Aled D
Flanagan, Sue	Rowlands, Eifion
Heaney, Rosemari	Simon, Catherine
Jones, Wendy	Spencer, Mair Elyned
Leahy, James	Voutsadakis, Mary
Leaney, Elanwy	Preston
Lloyd-Jones, Anita	Williams, Carol
Martin, Catherine	Williams, Doran
Morris, Alwena	Williams, Emyr
Myerscough, Bob	

Finally, respect to those whose contributions were more infrequent, but still very welcome:

Benbow, Megan
Brown, Janice
Cholomondeley, Keith
Cox, Lynda Mary
Davies, Ann
Davies, Elwyn
Dobbinskly, Pierre
Elizabeth, Carol
Ellul, Susan
Fairclough, Jane
Gardiner, Tim
Griffiths, Sheila
Hughes, Dave
Hughes, Eunice
Hughes, Sera
Humphries, Mandy
John-Thomas, David
Jones-Evans, Cyril
Jones, Arnold
Jones, Bethan
Jones, Catrin
Jones, Gail
Jones, Lisa
Jones, Lorna
Jones, Meira

Jones, Tim
Jones, Tony
Lewis, Dafydd
Linecar, Rhian
Massarelli, Stan
Mellor, Gweneth Lynes
Morgan, Joan
Parry, Gareth
Pritchard, Glen
Raymond-Jones, Gwenda
Roberts, Delyth
Roberts, Margaret
Robyns, Gwen
Scheel, Marion
Thomas, David John
Thomas, Renee Adewi
Trenholme, Carys
Vicary, Ann
Williams, Aled
Williams, Dilwyn
Williams, Gwen
Williams, John
Williams, Sarah
Wyn-Jones, Mario

Apologies if I've missed anybody out, or misspelled names – easily done over two years!

At other north Wales Facebook groups: To all those at Facebook groups Old Pictures of Pwllheli and Hiraeth Gogledd Cymru and a growing group of others who 'liked' my pictures, many taken twenty years ago and told me where I'd taken them.

Also:

- To Simon van de Put, for again allowing me to use, on the front cover and free of charge, one of his beautiful paintings of Pwllheli.
- To all the friends and acquaintances of my childhood – I hope you don't mind being mentioned by name, and that your families enjoy the stories (if they hadn't heard them already!).
- To my children (Daniel and Catherine) and grandchildren (Lazaros, Niko and Marlo), who enlivened the photographs of our numerous family holidays in north Wales, and chipped in with some vivid memories.
- To my wife Doulla who, with good grace, put up with all my maudlin *hiraeth* and did a first invaluable read-through of the manuscript.
- To my brother and fellow author Chris who gave me not only encouragement, but also a younger perspective and a wealth of stories that he'd picked up from our mother after I'd flown the nest.
- To friends in Newcastle-under-Lyme who have encouraged me, especially Brian Smith who bought me a fine copy of *In Search of Wales* and Steve Meys who told me things about the maternal side of my family that even my mother didn't know.
- Above all, to the people of Llŷn in general, and Pwllheli in particular, for giving me such a memorable childhood and, hopefully, for buying this book in huge numbers!

Also by the author:

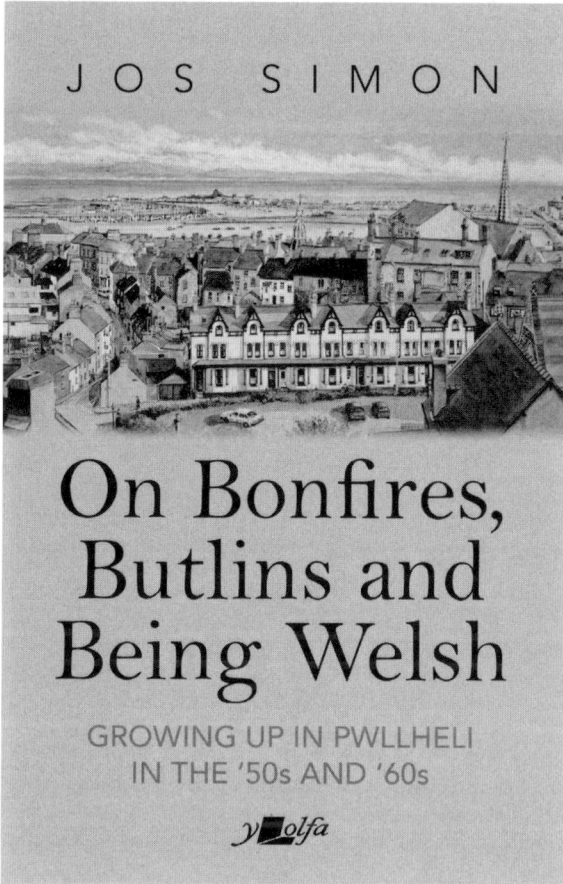

J O S   S I M O N

On Bonfires,
Butlins and
Being Welsh

GROWING UP IN PWLLHELI
IN THE '50s AND '60s

y Lolfa

£9.99

Also from Y Lolfa:

RICHARD RHYS O'BRIEN

The Campaigns of
MARGARET LLOYD GEORGE
THE WIFE OF THE PRIME MINISTER 1916–1922

y Lolfa

£14.99

RICHARD RHYS O'BRIEN

*The Woman Who
Helped Win the War*

THE WELFARE CAMPAIGNS OF
MARGARET LLOYD GEORGE, 1914–1918

'A long overdue look at the woman
behind the great man' – DAN SNOW

y*olfa*

£19.99

Salem a Fi

ENDAF EMLYN

y olfa

£11.99